MEL BLACKABY
and BO STEVENS

LifeWay Press®
Nashville, Tennessee

ISBN 978-1-4158-6548-4
Item 005085766

Dewey decimal classification: 248.84.0
Subject heading: DISCIPLESHIP \ CHURCH \ CHRISTIAN LIFE

This book is the resource for course CG-1257 in the subject area The Church in the Christian Growth Study Plan.

Cover illustration: Mac Premo

To order additional copies of this resource, write to LifeWay Church Resources Customer Service; One LifeWay Plaza; Nashville, TN 37234-0113; fax (615) 251-5933; phone toll free (800) 458-2772; e-mail *orderentry@lifeway.com;* order online at *www.lifeway.com;* or visit the LifeWay Christian Store serving you.

Printed in the United States of America

Leadership and Adult Publishing
LifeWay Church Resources
One LifeWay Plaza
Nashville, TN 37234-0175

Contents

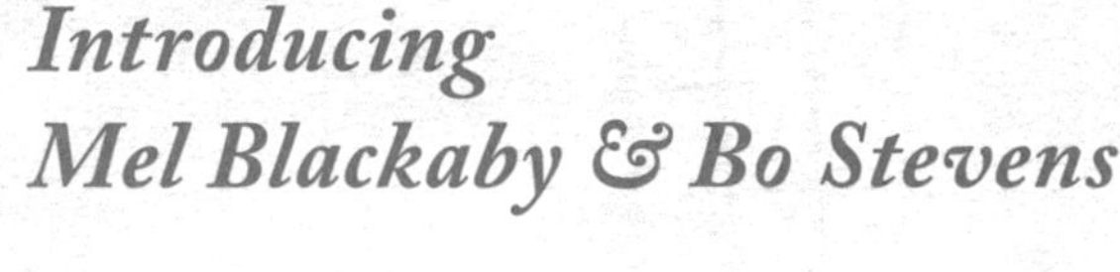

Introducing Mel Blackaby & Bo Stevens

Mel Blackaby is the senior pastor of First Baptist Church in Jonesboro, Georgia. During the time he wrote this book, he was serving as the senior pastor of Bow Valley Baptist Church in Cochrane, Alberta, Canada. He has also served as the senior pastor of churches in Bluff Dale, Texas, and Kamloops, British Columbia, Canada. Mel earned a bachelor of arts from Hardin-Simmons University and a master of divinity and doctor of philosophy from Southwestern Baptist Theological Seminary in Fort Worth, Texas.

Mel is the author of *Going the Second Mile* and has cowritten numerous books with his father, Henry Blackaby, including *A God-Centered Church, Your Church Experiencing God Together, What's So Spiritual About Your Gifts?* and *Experiencing the Resurrection.* He was also a contributor to *The Blackaby Study Bible.* Mel and his wife, Gina, have three children: Christa, Stephen, and Sarah. They enjoy riding horses in the mountains, traveling, and just hanging out as a family.

Bo Stevens is the pastor of discipleship and administration at Bow Valley Baptist Church in Cochrane, Alberta, Canada. He earned a bachelor of business administration from Southern Arkansas University in Magnolia, Arkansas, and both a master of divinity and master of religious education from the Canadian Southern Baptist Seminary in Cochrane, Alberta, Canada.

Bo developed *Growing Disciples: Abide in Christ,* using a classic Andrew Murray text. He has developed other material for new believers and is helping them grow in their new faith. God is using Bo in the United States and Canada to speak in churches and conferences. He and his wife, Tonya, live in Cochrane with their three children: Lauren, Paige, and Cody.

Preface

God's gift of salvation is not just the guarantee of eternity in heaven; it is also an expression of God's desire to bring you into the family of God. In fact, His primary goal is for you to enter a love relationship with Him and His people.

As I travel and speak within the Christian community, I am astounded to see how often God's people are disoriented to His original purpose for their lives. Their frustration with the Christian life usually comes from a misunderstanding of the interdependent relationship believers have with one another. Jesus told us to give ourselves away for the sake of the body; yet many believers don't want to get involved in the church and protect themselves at all cost. That maverick attitude is totally opposed to the plan of God. He does not want those who are born again to live as spiritual orphans but as members of His family. Outside that family relationship, the Christian life cannot be lived as God planned. Believers don't have the spiritual resources within ourselves to grow and mature without the rest of the body of Christ.

Our prayer is that you will seek genuine fellowship with believers as a necessary step in your journey with Christ. And in that fellowship you will experience life more abundant and full. In a healthy relationship with the family of God, you will be in a position to see and experience Him working in our world in a way that is beyond your wildest imagination. For the church is God's strategy to touch the world with the power of the gospel.

To God be the glory,

Mel Blackaby

Introducing Fellowship with Believers

Growing Disciples: Fellowship with Believers is part of the Growing Disciples Series (see p. 110). This series of self-paced, interactive Bible studies introduces you to six disciplines illustrated by the Disciple's Cross that was first developed and popularized by Avery Willis in *MasterLife: A Biblical Process for Growing Disciples.* Take a look at the diagram of the Disciple's Cross below to see where the discipline of Fellowship with Believers fits in the spiritual life of a follower of Jesus Christ.

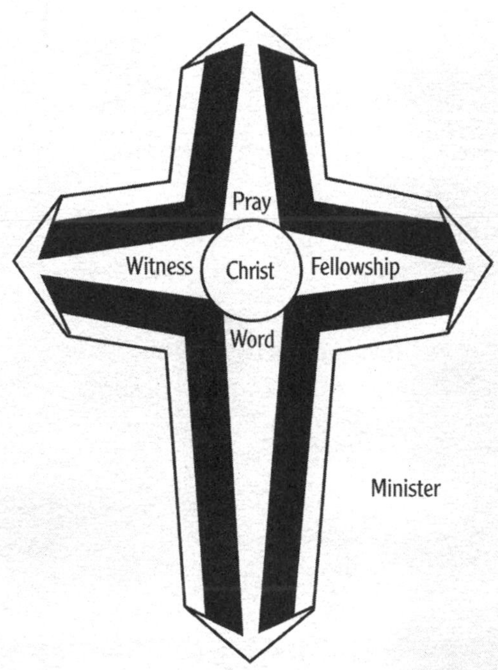

Fellowship with believers is one of the disciplines in the crossbar designating your relationships with others—in this case, with other believers. This fellowship grows from a relationship with Jesus Christ, which is a prerequisite for all the other disciplines. As we begin the study of this discipline, let's first take a brief look at all six.

The Six Disciplines of the Disciple's Cross

1. ABIDE IN CHRIST

To abide in Christ is central to all of the disciplines. Jesus invites you to a love relationship with Himself. He wants you to know, understand, and live according to His commands so that you can experience the best life God has to offer you. His Word and prayer are the tools through which we speak to Him and He speaks to us. By abiding in Christ, you receive all the life and vitality you need to be filled with joy and fruitfulness.

2. LIVE IN THE WORD

God has revealed Himself, His purposes, and His ways in the Bible. He has given guidelines for an abundant and meaningful life. Jesus set an example for us by knowing Scripture and applying it in His daily living. You will learn to read, study, memorize, and meditate on God's Word in order to know Him and understand His commands, His purposes, and His ways. Then you can live your life in a way that pleases Him and is abundantly full.

3. PRAY IN FAITH

Prayer is not just a religious activity; it describes a relationship with a person. Prayer is your intimate communion with God. In prayer you experience a loving relationship, you receive God's counsel and directions, you respond in praise and worship, you receive cleansing through confession, and you work together with God through petition for yourself and intercession for others.

4. FELLOWSHIP WITH BELIEVERS

When Jesus saved you, He placed you in the body of Christ with other believers. In relationships with other believers, you receive help to be all God wants you to be; and God uses you to meet the needs of the rest of the body. Together we grow strong in our faith, and we accomplish the kingdom work of Christ in the world for which He died.

5. WITNESS TO THE WORLD

Jesus came with an assignment to seek and to save those who are lost. He went to the cross to reconcile a lost world to God the Father. He has given to us the ministry and message of reconciliation so that others can experience a saving relationship with God. We have both the privilege and the responsibility to witness about Christ to a lost and dying world around us.

6. MINISTER TO OTHERS

Jesus modeled a life of service for His disciples and for us. He did not come to be served but to serve others. His call for us is to a life of service to those who are needy, both in the body of Christ and in the world that has yet to believe. When we love and serve others who are needy, we show our love for Christ Himself; and God uses that service to build up the body of Christ.

The Growing Disciples Series provides a six-week study for each of the six disciplines in the Disciple's Cross. *The Call to Follow Christ,* the first book in the series, introduces the six disciplines for new and growing believers. Though you would benefit from studying that course first, it is not a prerequisite. A person can study the individual disciplines in any order, based on interest and spiritual need. The goal of discipleship is to grow strong and balanced in each of these six disciplines. Because new believers need to understand the importance of belonging to and functioning in the body of Christ, this can be a valuable study whether it comes first or later.

Small-Group Study of *Fellowship with Believers*

When God saved you, He placed you in the body of Christ so that you can benefit from the ministry of the other members of the body. You are also in the body to help others. The writer of Hebrews instructs us, "Let us consider how we may spur one another on toward love and good deeds. Let us not give up meeting together, as some are in the habit of doing, but let us encourage one another" (Hebrews 10:24-25, NIV). That's what this particular course will help you experience. Join a group of other believers in Christ. If necessary, enlist some to join you in your study so that you can help one another grow in following Christ. You will find that we need one another, and we can help one another grow in Christ.

If you are the person who will lead the small-group sessions, we've included a brief leader guide, beginning on page 106. Guides for each small-group session appear at the end of each week's daily devotionals so that all group members will have access to the questions and sharing activities.

Personal Study of *Fellowship with Believers*

This book may be different from others you have read. This is a self-paced, interactive study. We're not just speaking to you as we write. We want you to interact with us and with the Lord, so we will give you instructions for at least two types of activities.

One is a prayer activity that begins with an arrow pointing up to God and down to you. The arrow symbolizes what we want you to do in prayer: talk to the Lord and listen as He speaks to you. At the beginning of each day we will ask you to listen to God through His Word; you'll read a Scripture verse or two from the Bible. Then we'll ask you to meditate and pray. At other times we will give you suggestions for a time of prayer. Take a moment right now to pray and ask God to guide you and speak to you as you pray to Him over the next six weeks.

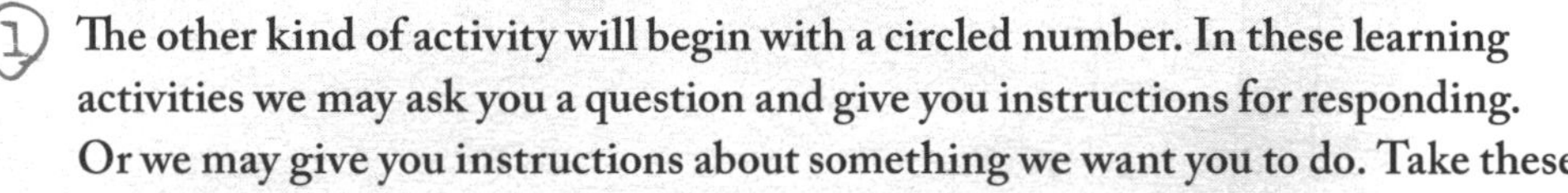

The other kind of activity will begin with a circled number. In these learning activities we may ask you a question and give you instructions for responding. Or we may give you instructions about something we want you to do. Take these

learning activities seriously. Don't skip over them to move on in your reading. We don't want you just to read some information about following Christ. We want you to understand the message, and we want you to apply it to your life and your relationship with the body of Christ. These learning activities will help you understand and apply these truths to your life. Will you work with us by completing these learning activities? Check your response: ○ Yes ○ No

We hope you answered yes. If you answered no, you'll miss much of the help this study can provide for your spiritual growth. After the learning activities we may give you some feedback about your response, as we're doing now. If there are correct answers, we will provide them either in the following paragraph or in the margin.

Each week you will study five daily lessons before getting together with a mentor or a small group to process what you are leaning. Don't wait until the end of the week to start your study. We don't want you to be overwhelmed by having too much to do in too short a time. That can be discouraging. But more importantly, we want you to develop a habit of spending time with God every day. Some people call this a quiet time or devotional time. Take some time every day (preferably at the beginning of the day) to read God's Word, study or meditate on its meaning, and talk to God in prayer. For the next six weeks let this book be your guide. By starting the day with your focus on God and His Word, you will be in a position all day to let God apply the truths to your life. As you do this in "chewable bites" (small pieces at a time), you will learn and grow at a reasonable pace. You will need to study week 1 before your first small-group session unless your leader instructs you otherwise.

We also want you to memorize some Bible verses. These Scriptures can guide you, encourage you, warn you, or give you a promise from God to keep in your mind. We've chosen a verse for each week that will apply to the topic for the week.

(2) **Turn to the back of the book and tear out the Scripture-memory cards. Use one each week to memorize the assigned verse and review the verses from previous weeks.**

Note: Because of the way we've written this study, we will frequently use the first-person pronouns *I* and *me*. If we're sharing a personal illustration when we think you'd like to know, we'll identify which author is speaking (Mel or Bo).

Week 1

Born into the Family of God

"Jesus answered and said to him, 'Most assuredly, I say to you, unless one is born again, he cannot see the kingdom of God.' "

John 3:3

Born into the Family of God

OVERVIEW OF WEEK 1

Day 1: The Joy of New Birth
Day 2: Chosen by God
Day 3: Children Need God's Family
Day 4: Children Mature in God's Family
Day 5: Personal but Not Private

VERSE TO MEMORIZE

"Look at how great a love the Father has given us, that we should be called God's children" (1 John 3:1).

DISCIPLESHIP HELP FOR WEEK 1

"Are You in the Family?" (pp. 94–95)
"Born Again" (p. 96)

POSSIBLE RESPONSES TO WEEK 1

As I come to understand and appreciate what belonging to God's family can mean to me, I will respond by doing things like the following.

- I will take time this week to thank persons the Lord used to bring me to salvation.
- I will allow the Lord to shape my life so that it bears fruit for His honor and glory.
- I will ask the Lord to lead me to persons in my church to whom I can express His love in practical ways.
- I will seek to do all the Lord shows me in order to grow and mature in my relationship with Him.
- I will be more committed to my church family because God expects me to express His love to them.

Day 1 • The Joy of New Birth

God's Word for Today

"Look at how great a love the Father has given us, that we should be called God's children." 1 John 3:1

Today's Spiritual Reality

To be born again is to be a member of God's family.

Luke 15:7

"I tell you, in the same way, there will be more joy in heaven over one sinner who repents than over 99 righteous people who don't need repentance."

John 1:12-13

"To all who did receive Him, He gave them the right to be children of God, to those who believe in His name, who were born, not of blood, or of the will of the flesh, or of the will of man, but of God."

Ephesians 2:19

"You are no longer foreigners and strangers, but fellow citizens with the saints, and members of God's household."

Read and meditate on "God's Word for Today" and "Today's Spiritual Reality" in the margin. Begin today's study with prayer.

Nothing equals the joy of a new baby's arrival—the wonder of creation, the delight of seeing a son or daughter for the first time, and the anticipation of what dynamics the child will bring into the family. But the joy of physical birth that gives temporal life cannot compare to the joy of spiritual birth, which gives eternal life. In fact, Jesus said all heaven rejoices over one person who repents of his sin and is born into the family of God (see Luke 15:7). Can you believe it? Christians are in the family of God!

1. **Turn to page 94 and take the self-test "Are You in the Family?" to help you determine whether you are a member of God's family.**

From this point forward we're going to write with the assumption that you are already a member of God's family.

Jesus' words in John 3 are much more than a figure of speech; they are a spiritual reality: "I assure you: Unless someone is born again, he cannot see the kingdom of God" (John 3:3). Jesus went on to explain, "Whatever is born of the flesh is flesh, and whatever is born of the Spirit is spirit" (John 3:6). Just as we are physically born into the human race, Christians are spiritually born into the family of God.

2. **Read the following verses in the margins. Then match the reference on the left with the description of what happens when a person becomes a Christian. Write one or more letters beside each reference.**

____ John 1:12-13	a. I became a member of God's household/family.
____ Ephesians 2:19	b. I was adopted by God, my spiritual Father.
____ Romans 8:15	c. I became a child of God.
	d. I became a fellow citizen with the other saints.

God is much more than a Creator, King, or Master. He is a Heavenly Father who cares for those He adopts into His family. If you are His child, you are part of His family. Does that overwhelm you? God loves you. He chose and adopted you!

The joy of new birth, however, is not reserved for heaven alone; there is also much rejoicing on earth. A larger family was impacted when you were spiritually reborn. Salvation probably did not happen in isolation but was the culmination of God's working through other people to draw you to Himself. Some prayed, some touched your life through acts of kindness, some met a need through ministry, some shared the gospel, while others just loved you.

Romans 8:15
"You did not receive a spirit of slavery to fall back into fear, but you received the Spirit of adoption, by whom we cry out, 'Abba, Father!' "

3. **Thank God for those who helped you come to Christ and take time this week to thank each of them for his or her influence in your life.**

____

#2 answers: John 1:12-13 (c); Ephesians 2:19 (a, d); Romans 8:15 (b)

Paul wrote that we should joyfully give thanks for all God has done in our lives (see Colossians 1:11-14). Never lose the joy of your salvation. Never view your faith as commonplace or ordinary. Salvation is nothing less than a miracle of God.

Colossians 1:11-14
"With joy giv[e] thanks to the Father, who has enabled you to share in the saints' inheritance in the light. He has rescued us from the domain of darkness and transferred us into the kingdom of the Son He loves, in whom we have redemption, the forgiveness of sins."

When you fully understand the nature of salvation and your birth into the family of God, you will know and experience the joy of the Lord. It springs from a newfound confidence in life that is rooted in faith—a keen awareness that the living Lord is present in your life. In the Bible, joy is much more than an emotion or a feeling; it is the ability to see beyond any particular situation to the sovereign Lord, who stands above all circumstances and ultimately has control over them. He provides the family of God as the context in which we can enjoy our salvation.

The New Testament frequently uses family images to refer to Christians, with words like *born, children, brothers, Father,* and *household of faith*. When you realize that these terms are not just word pictures but spiritual realities, your relationship with God will take on a whole new meaning. So now that you are in the family, take a look around. You have a large family that is waiting to meet you. In fact, all believers worldwide are now "blood relatives" in Christ Jesus.

Conclude today's lesson by talking with God about your new birth. Express your gratitude to Him for what He has done in your life. If you realize you have never experienced this new birth, turn to "Born Again" on page 96 and consider receiving this wonderful gift God offers you.

Day 2 • Chosen by God

Read and meditate on "God's Word for Today" and "Today's Spiritual Reality" in the margin. Begin today's study with prayer.

God's Word for Today

"To all who did receive Him, He gave them the right to be children of God, to those who believe in His name, who were born, not of blood, or of the will of the flesh, or of the will of man, but of God." John 1:12-13

Today's Spiritual Reality

God has chosen you to be in His family.

John 6:44
"No one can come to Me unless the Father who sent Me draws him, and I will raise him up on the last day."

Romans 8:29
"Those He foreknew He also predestined to be conformed to the image of His Son, so that He would be the firstborn among many brothers."

One amazing aspect of salvation is that God chose to save you. His love for you compelled Him to reach down and bring you into His family. He drew you to Himself (John 6:44). Your salvation was not an accident. God willed for you to be born into His family. Jesus said, "You did not choose Me, but I chose you" (John 15:16). You then responded to His choosing you by receiving the gift of salvation He provided.

1. **Read Romans 8:29 in the margin and answer the following statements *T* for *true* and *F* for *false*.**
   ___ 1. God has known me from the very beginning.
   ___ 2. God doesn't have a plan for me, so I need to come up with one.
   ___ 3. God's purpose is for me to look and act like Jesus.

From the very beginning, God chose to bring you into His family and to allow you to enjoy the benefits of that relationship. He wanted you to be conformed to the image of His Son and to be connected to His family.

God's plan to bring you into the middle of His activity means He has a plan for your life. In other words, we don't come to Him with our dreams for what we want to accomplish. Rather, He wants to conform us to the image He has for us—the image of Christ. To experience the fullness of God's great salvation, we must yield our lives to His will. His will begins with our being involved in God's family.

Consider 1 Corinthians 12:18: "God has set the members, each one of them, in the body just as He pleased" (NKJV). Later in this study we will talk about how we fit into the body of Christ, the church; but for now just consider the fact that God has placed you into the body as it pleased Him. He wants to do something *through* you to build up the body, and He wants to do something *in* you through other members of the body.

Being chosen by God is not just a privilege but also a responsibility. We are responsible for fulfilling the purpose for which He chose us. We naturally

#1 answers: 1-T, 2-F, 3-T

tend to be very self-centered, but we need to be God-centered. He did not choose us just so that we could enjoy the good life, lavished with heavenly blessings. No, to be chosen by God means He has something in mind for our lives, a purpose for us to fulfill. There are blessings, and there is a wonderful love relationship with God … but there is much more.

John 15:16
"You did not choose Me, but I chose you. I appointed you that you should go out and produce fruit and that your fruit should remain, so that whatever you ask the Father in My name, He will give you."

2. **Read John 15:16 in the margin and underline the statement that reflects what God expected when He chose you.**

All believers want their lives to be fruitful. But we need to understand what kind of fruit God is looking for. Spiritual fruit is not produced through great effort. It is the result of being connected to Christ and functioning where He placed us. John 15:5 reminds us that we need to remain in Christ in order to bear fruit. God's call is first and foremost a call to a love relationship; so if you are not living in that relationship, you cannot experience a fruitful life. A love relationship with Him will always lead to obedience. Obedience will result in fruit that will last.

John 15:5, NKJV
"I am the vine, you are the branches. He who abides in Me, and I in him, bears much fruit; for without Me you can do nothing."

3. **Number the following experiences in proper order from 1 (first) to 3 (third).**

___ a. Bearing spiritual fruit
___ b. Obedience
___ c. Love relationship

#2 answer: produce fruit
#3 answers a-3, b-2, c-1

The essence of obedience is not necessarily doing right but being right. That is, you must become who God wants you to be, which will result in right action. Salvation is being in right relationship with God and His family. In that relationship you will experience abundant life. Outside this right relationship there is nothing you can do that will please God, for that would mean you are out of His will and are acting contrary to His very nature. As you grow in your faith, pursue healthy relationships with the family of God. God does His greatest work in and through the family.

God does His greatest work in and through the family.

Conclude today's lesson by thanking the Lord for choosing you and placing you in His body—for adding you to His family. Pray that God will shape you to function in it just as He desires. Ask Him to enable your obedience so that you can bear spiritual fruit for Him.

Day 3 • Children Need God's Family

Read and meditate on "God's Word for Today" and "Today's Spiritual Reality" in the margin. Begin today's study with prayer.

God's Word for Today
"By obedience to the truth, having purified yourselves for sincere love of the brothers, love one another earnestly from a pure heart, since you have been born again—not of perishable seed but of imperishable—through the living and enduring word of God." 1 Peter 1:22-23

Today's Spiritual Reality
God expects His children to love His family.

A young family in our church went through a very difficult time. The husband had sold a successful business in order to enter seminary and prepare for a life of service. The family included four boys who were six years old and younger. The mother, however, began to suffer from a debilitating, degenerative illness. The only solution was experimental surgery that could be performed only in a special hospital on the other side of the country at great financial cost.

The couple felt overwhelmed as the financial, emotional, and spiritual needs of their situation mounted. During times like these, people need to be part of God's family—the church. The body of Christ demonstrated their love for this family by providing child care, doing laundry, cleaning the house, preparing meals, and offering other means of support. Prayer for the family grew as the entire church rallied to address the crisis. This was not *their* problem to deal with; it was *our* problem. *They* were not hurting alone; *we* were hurting. Together we sought the Lord for help. And together we experienced God's amazing love and provision.

The apostle Paul said, "If one member suffers, all the members suffer with it; or if one member is honored, all the members rejoice with it" (1 Corinthians 12:26). To be connected to the people of God brings your life into the care of God's family. I can't imagine this family going through their crisis alone. That is why God surrounded us with a church family to love and care for one another. When you were born again, you were born into a family. As a natural result of being born again, we develop a sincere love for the family of God. The salvation experience and fellowship with believers go hand in hand. God's great salvation places you in an environment in which you receive all you need to grow and mature spiritually.

God's great salvation places you in an environment in which you receive all you need to grow and mature spiritually.

1. **Up until now, which of the following would best describe your identification with the family of God? Check one.**
   a. I've learned to suffer and rejoice with other members of God's family.
   b. I've been more emotionally isolated from members of God's family.

If a baby were born and left to herself without anyone to care for her, what would life be like? Would she enjoy life? Could she even survive? A baby does not have the capacity to care for herself. The potential is there, but the ability is not yet developed. God designed the human family as the best place for a child to grow and mature. The parents feed her, pick her up when she falls, teach her, and love her. The investment of the parents has a great impact on the future of that child. Without them, the child cannot know life as God intended her to know it.

The same thing is true spiritually. God desires for every person who has been born again to experience life at its best. To do so, they must be intimately involved in the family of God. They must be connected to a church that will feed them, pick them up when they fall, teach them, and love them. Salvation is not just personal; it has a corporate (group) dimension to it as well. The corporate dimension of salvation is essential if you are to realize your potential as a child of God. Just as no human family is perfect, no church family is perfect. Yet God has perfectly designed the church to help you grow in your faith and experience abundant life in Christ.

God has perfectly designed the church to help you grow in your faith and experience abundant life in Christ.

The decision to be part of a church family not only benefits your spiritual growth but also reflects your love for the Heavenly Father. Even more, it is part of the evidence that you are truly born again. Jesus said, "By this all people will know that you are My disciples, if you have love for one another" (John 13:35). God is love, and His children reflect His nature.

1 John 4:7-8
"Dear friends, let us love one another, because love is from God, and everyone who loves has been born of God and knows God. The one who does not love does not know God, because God is love."

2. **Read 1 John 4:7-8 in the margin and fill in the blanks below.**
   a. The evidence that we are born of God is that we ________________.
   b. If we do not love one another, we do not ________________ God.

3. **Are you expressing your love for God by loving His family?**
   ○ Yes ○ No ○ Sometimes

Ask the Lord to help you love others in the body of Christ.

Conclude today's lesson by talking with God about what He knows you need from the family of God. Ask Him what He wants to do in your life through the family that will help you mature spiritually. Ask Him how He wants you to contribute to the growth of others.

#2 answers: a–love, b–know

Day 4 • Children Mature in God's Family

God's Word for Today
"Those He foreknew He also predestined to be conformed to the image of His Son, so that He would be the firstborn among many brothers."
Romans 8:29

Today's Spiritual Reality
Healthy children always grow and mature.

Read and meditate on "God's Word for Today" and "Today's Spiritual Reality" in the margin. Begin today's study with prayer.

My (Mel's) firstborn child was a little girl named Christa. Her birth had complications; but by the end of the day we held a beautiful, healthy girl. She was perfect in every way, and our joy was complete. But imagine if she had never grown. How would we have felt a year later if she had weighed just six pounds? Why would we have been full of sorrow if Christa had weighed exactly the same one year later? It is because we expect children to grow and mature. It is a natural part of life.

Infants are not expected to contribute anything to the family except their presence. They don't do the dishes, take out the garbage, or even engage in meaningful conversations. They have just been born! Although they are full of potential, they do not yet have the capacity to help with the affairs of the home. But as time goes on, they are expected to grow and become contributing members of the family.

We are meant to grow into Christlikeness, not stay the same.

The same is true of those born into the family of God. As exciting as it is for people to be born again and enter the family, they have just started the journey. They have great potential, but it is yet to be realized. They need to be nurtured and cared for by other family members.

Ephesians 4:14-15
"We will no longer be little children, tossed by the waves and blown around by every wind of teaching, by human cunning with cleverness in the techniques of deceit. But speaking the truth in love, let us grow in every way into Him who is the head—Christ."

God intended all Christians to be conformed to the image of His Son (Romans 8:29). That suggests a maturing process. We are meant to grow into Christlikeness, not stay the same (see Ephesians 4:14-15). To be "born" is the first step among many that lie before new believers. New Christians should not expect to act like mature Christians but should strive to learn from such people and expect the Lord to help them grow in spiritual maturity.

What should you expect as a Christian? Select one.
○ a. To stay the same
○ **b.** To grow and mature in Christ

#1 answer: b

That's obvious, isn't it? God wants you to grow. As much as new Christians need a church family to help them grow, they reach a point when they want to help others grow in their faith. It is not all about receiving; you must also give. The longer you have been a Christian, the more will be expected from your life.

One joy of being a pastor is watching believers mature in their faith. Over the years we have seen many young people follow God's call to full-time Christian service. I'm often amazed as I look back on their lives. One such person was Michael. I remember when he was a child running through the church, when as a teenager he dyed his hair exotic colors, and when he was part of a band that played loud music and sang words that could be understood only with "special gifts of discernment." But I also remember Michael's tender heart toward God. I think of the many friends he brought to our youth group and the way he faithfully came every Sunday to worship God. Then there was the day he became part of our adult praise team that led our church in worshiping God. Who knew? But that is not all. Michael taught in our Vacation Bible School, he was selected to preach on Youth Sunday, he served as a summer missionary, he pursued studies in seminary, and he asked whether he could go visiting with me so that he could learn to share the gospel. It was a great moment when I sat beside Michael the first time he led someone to pray and receive Christ as Savior and Lord.

Was I surprised? No, I expect every new believer to grow up and serve the Lord. Not everyone will be a pastor or a church leader, but every child of God should mature in his or her faith and contribute to the family of God.

Every child of God should mature in his or her faith and contribute to the family of God.

As you think about being part of the body of Christ, don't just look at who you are or what you have been. Consider who you will be and the purpose of your life. Strive to grow in the relationship and watch God transform you into the image of His Son. Enjoy being a child of God, but don't remain childish. Grow up and experience a mature walk with Christ.

Which describes your growth in Christ over the past year? Circle one.

Much growth   Some growth   No growth

Conclude today's lesson by talking with God about your spiritual growth. Think of the people He has placed in your life to help you grow as His child. Thank the Lord for giving you these people. Pray that He will use you to help others grow in Him.

Day 5 • Personal but Not Private

Read and meditate on "God's Word for Today" and "Today's Spiritual Reality" in the margin. Begin today's study with prayer.

God's Word for Today

"By this all people will know that you are My disciples, if you have love for one another." John 13:35

Today's Spiritual Reality

Genuine salvation is visible for all to see.

We often talk about a personal walk with God through Jesus Christ. That understanding is correct. Jesus' death and resurrection brought forgiveness of sin and direct access to our holy God. As a result, we enjoy a relationship that is unique, intimate, and personal. But never assume that personal means private; nothing could be further from the truth.

Do not equate spiritual matters with the terms *invisible, unseen,* or *private;* for the Spirit-filled life is obvious to all who see it. The Bible describes Christians as the salt of the earth, a lamp that gives light in a dark world, and a city set on a hill that all can see (see Matthew 5:13-15). Jesus did not say we *have* salt or light. He said we *are* salt and light and, by our very nature, will impact everybody we encounter. Jesus challenges every believer to confess Him as Lord publicly and to live for Him openly for all to see.

Matthew 5:13-15
"You are the salt of the earth. But if the salt should lose its taste, how can it be made salty? It's no longer good for anything but to be thrown out and trampled on by men. You are the light of the world. A city situated on a hill cannot be hidden. No one lights a lamp and puts it under a basket, but rather on a lampstand, and it gives light for all who are in the house."

Our faith is personal but never private. We cannot live our faith in isolation; that would run contrary to the purpose of God's salvation. No one in the Bible had a relationship with God in private. Rather, each had significant involvement with God's people, for that is where God's heart is found.

1. **Our relationship with Christ should be (check all that apply)—**
   ○ a. private ○ b. unseen ○ c. visible
   ○ d. personal ○ e. impacting to others ○ f. obvious

#1 answers: c, d, e, f

Some people talk about their love for God but have no connection to the people of God. When challenged to be part of a church, they claim, "My relationship with God is personal." That statement is an excuse meaning "I don't want to get involved." It runs contrary to the heart of what being a Christian means.

2. **Reread John 13:35 in the margin ("God's Word for Today") and answer the following questions.**
   a. Who will know you are Jesus' disciple? ____________________
   b. How will they know you are Jesus' disciple? ____________________

#2 answers: a–all/everyone, b–love for one another

God is concerned that we have a love relationship with His family. He values a love relationship with Him and a love relationship with one another. In fact, if you are not walking in love relationships with other believers, there is a great question whether you are in fact a Christian.

If you are not walking in love relationships with other believers, there is a great question whether you are in fact a Christian.

(3) **As you read 1 John 3:14 in the margin, circle the indicator that someone has passed from death to life. Underline the indicator that someone is still in death.**

1 John 3:14
"We know that we have passed from death to life because we love our brothers. The one who does not love remains in death."

If I reworded 1 John 4:20-21 in a succinct statement and applied it to your life, I would say one evidence you are a child of God is that you love the people of God. Can you confidently say before God that you love those who are in His family? Your answer may very well reveal whether you have been born again by the Spirit of God.

1 John 4:20-21
"If anyone says, 'I love God,' yet hates his brother, he is a liar. For the person who does not love his brother whom he has seen cannot love God whom he has not seen. And we have this command from Him: the one who loves God must also love his brother."

As a pastor, I (Mel) don't get too worried if Christians lack Bible knowledge. That can be taught in sermons and Bible study classes. I am not upset when they have a different view on certain theological issues. Some topics will be sorted out only when we see the Lord face-to-face. But one thing that does concern me is a person who is unloving. It shows me his heart. I'm concerned when a person pulls away from the people of God and refuses to be in relationship with them. I'm concerned when a person is easily offended or angered at God's people. A person who has been born of God will demonstrate the love of God with the people of God.

Let me reemphasize that a relationship with God is personal but not private. That is why this study is so important. Your fellowship with believers is crucial if you want to experience abundant life in Christ. Remember, you were born into a family; and God expects you to function as a responsible, contributing member of that family.

Responding to the Lord

Take time to pray, asking the Lord to reveal whether you truly love His people. Ask Him to show you practical ways to love them.

Review this week's lessons and underline the statement or Scripture God seemed to emphasize to you the most. Ask the Lord to show you how He wants you to respond to Him and to His people in light of what He has said to you this week. Write in the margin a prayer of response to the Lord.

Session 1 • Born into the Family of God

Use some or all of the following suggestions to guide your small-group experience this week.

Opening Prayer

Building Relationships

Share the following with your group.

1. Your name and basic information about your immediate family.
2. How did the Lord lead you to participate in this study? Or: Why do you think this study will be valuable to you?

Responding to Learning Activities

Share your responses to some or all of the following learning activities.

- Page 95, activity 7. Or if you have just trusted Christ in response to this week's study, tell the group about your decision. Invite a volunteer to pray and thank God for what He has done in bringing each of you into His family of faith.
- Page 16, activity 1. Why?
- Page 19, activity 2. Why?

Reviewing Week 1

1. In pairs or triads take turns reciting your Scripture-memory verse, 1 John 3:1.
2. Leader: Using the diagram on page 6, briefly review the six disciplines of the Disciple's Cross to help members see where *Fellowship with Believers* fits into a well-rounded life of following Christ.
3. Review this week's daily spiritual realities, reproduced below. Which one do you think identifies a reality you and your church most need to develop more fully so that you will experience God's best as a fellowship of believers? Why?
   - Day 1: To be born again is to be a member of God's family.
   - Day 2: God has chosen you to be in His family.
   - Day 3: God expects His children to love His family.
   - Day 4: Healthy children always grow and mature.
   - Day 5: Genuine salvation is visible for all to see.

4. What are some ways a person can know he or she is in the faith (p. 94)?
5. What are the fruit of the Spirit that will be shown in the life of a person in whom the Spirit of Christ lives (pp. 94–95)?
6. What happens when a person becomes a Christian? What does God do (p. 12, activity 2)?
7. What are two prerequisites for bearing spiritual fruit (p. 15, activity 3)?
8. Why do you think God places His children in a family relationship with other believers (days 3–4)?
9. How will people know you and your church are disciples of Jesus Christ (p. 20, activity 2)?
10. Why is a private faith that is separate from the family of God (the body of Christ) *not* God's plan for believers (day 5)?

Building Up the Body

1. During your review at the end of day 5, what statement or Scripture did you identify that you think God emphasized most this week?
2. Which truth that you have studied this week do you think would do the most to build up the body of Christ if you and other members of your church faithfully applied it?
3. How do you want to respond to what you have learned this week? How has the Lord prompted you this week to love His people and build up His body?

Praying Together

Volunteers, pray in the following ways.

1. Ask the Lord to draw each person closer to Him and His people. Pray for your group members that God will enable each of you to grow and mature as His children.
2. Pray specifically that your church family will allow the Lord to help you function together as His family, showing a family resemblance and loving one another.

Preview Week 2

Turn to page 25 and preview the study for the coming week.

Week 2

The Covenant

"Let us be concerned about one another in order to promote love and good works, not staying away from our meetings, as some habitually do, but encouraging each other, and all the more as you see the day drawing near."

Hebrews 10:24-25

The Covenant

OVERVIEW OF WEEK 2

Day 1: Membership
Day 2: Defining the Covenant
Day 3: Symbols of the Covenant
Day 4: Testing the Covenant
Day 5: Blessing in the Covenant

VERSE TO MEMORIZE

"Let us be concerned about one another in order to promote love and good works, not staying away from our meetings, as some habitually do, but encouraging each other, and all the more as you see the day drawing near" (Hebrews 10:24-25).

POSSIBLE RESPONSES TO WEEK 2

As I come to understand and appreciate the covenant relationship God intends the church to have, I will respond by doing things like the following.

- I will seek to live more committed and connected to my church family.
- I will look for ways to connect with new members and help them function in the church body.
- I will regularly confirm in my heart the covenant with Christ and the church.
- I want God to use me to build up His body in good times and in times of crisis. I will seek to find ways to support those in my church who face crises.
- I will express to the Lord and His people my commitment to live in covenant with Him and my church family.

Day 1 • Membership

Read and meditate on "God's Word for Today" and "Today's Spiritual Reality" in the margin. Begin today's study with prayer.

God's Word for Today
"God has set the members, each one of them, in the body just as He pleased."
1 Corinthians 12:18, NKJV

Today's Spiritual Reality
We are members of the body of Christ.

To be part of the family of God is a great privilege, but many people hesitate to become members of a local church. Some argue that they don't need to be a member of a church. Some even claim that church membership is unbiblical.

The early church knew exactly who was part of the church and who was not.

The early church knew exactly who was part of the church and who was not. Letters were written to churches in various cities. To whom did they send them? To specific people who composed the church. Church discipline was practiced, setting rebellious people outside the church. How could people have been removed from the church if there had been no official entrance into the church? The church was commanded to care for and disciple each one as God added them to the body. How did they know whom to care for and disciple? When giving instruction on the proper use of spiritual gifts, Paul wrote that because visitors may be present, members should behave in an orderly manner (see 1 Corinthians 14:22-40). A worship service will have people present who are members of that body and others who are not.

1. **Mark the following statements *T* for *true* or *F* for *false*.**
   ___ a. The early church knew who was a member and who was not.
   ___ b. Church membership is not important for Christians today.

The early church had not developed into denominations by the time the New Testament was written, and the congregations didn't have all the structures we have today. But they clearly knew who was a member of the church and who was not. They were committed to God and to one another. They were prepared to lay down their lives for the church. New believers were added to the church through baptism and a clear public statement of their faith. In Jewish thinking from days of old, a corporate identity was ingrained in the minds of the group. The early church had that same understanding of a close identity with the larger group.

God never intended for Christians to be independent, as if we could function all alone. Nor are we codependent, as if our relationship with God

#1 answers: a-T, b-F

were not enough. We are interdependent, created by God as social beings to work together for a common purpose. Every child of God has a strategic place designed by Him in the church. You belong!

Being a church member is not like being a member of a country club or a community organization. The term in the Bible is *member of the body*. Physically, each body has many members. Each one has a unique shape and a specific function, and each contributes to the overall well-being of the body. That is the image used in the Bible to describe the church.

Romans 12:5
"We who are many are one body in Christ and individually members of one another."

1 Corinthians 12:18-20
"God has placed the parts, each one of them, in the body just as He wanted. And if they were all the same part, where would the body be? Now there are many parts, yet one body."

(2) **Read the two passages in the margin. Then match the following statements on the left with the correct terms on the right.**

___ 1. The church is whose body?	a. Unique
___ 2. How many members are in the body?	b. Christ's
___ 3. Who put the members in the body?	c. God
___ 4. All members of the body are ______________.	d. Many

If you want to live to your fullest potential as a Christian, you need to function within the body of Christ. When we are connected, responding to the head, and working together, Christ has a healthy body through whom He can accomplish the Father's will.

When you are choosing a church to join, reflect on 1 Corinthians 12:18. The only reason to join a local body is that the Father adds you. Do not shop around for the church with the most dynamic worship service, the most exciting youth or children's program, or the largest congregation. Pray and ask the Father where He wants you to join. He may take you to a struggling church so that you can help it grow. Don't just consider what you desire; ask what His will is for your life and that of your family.

Don't just consider what you desire; ask what His will is for your life and that of your family.

(3) **Are you as connected to your church body as God desires? Ask Him how you can be more connected. Write one way below.**

____

____

Conclude today's lesson by talking with God about your church and those who are members. Pray that God will give your church a proper understanding of what being a member means.

#2 answers: 1-b, 2-d, 3-c, 4-a

Day 2 • Defining the Covenant

God's Word for Today

"Let us hold on to the confession of our hope without wavering, for He who promised is faithful." Hebrews 10:23

Today's Spiritual Reality

Fellowship in the church is based on a trust relationship.

Read and meditate on "God's Word for Today" and "Today's Spiritual Reality" in the margin. Begin today's study with prayer.

To join a local church is to enter a covenant. It is not just an act of joining a human organization. A covenant* is a sacred pledge based on trust between two parties. The trust relationship is the most significant component of a covenant. A contract is a legal obligation, a commitment is a promised word to keep, but a covenant is based on a trust relationship. That's why biblical marriages are first and foremost a covenant. As Christians, we enter a covenant with God, based on trust and received through faith; it is always initiated by God to accomplish His purposes.

covenant: a sacred pledge based on trust between two parties

1. **Which statement best describes the term *covenant?***
   - ○ a. Legal obligation
   - ○ b. A human promise
   - ○ c. Sacred pledge based on trust
   - ○ d. Signed contract

I have noticed an alarming trend in society that it is impacting the church. People are walking away from their contracts, commitments, and covenants, feeling no responsibility to those with whom they made agreements.

This happens in families. A man and a woman stand before each other and God and solemnly commit to love, cherish, and remain faithful until they part at death. But when hardship comes, they walk away, destroying a marriage and severely wounding a family.

This trend of walking away from commitments also happens among Christians. God gloriously saves someone from sin, gives them new life in the family of God, and adds them to a church body. Yet they casually leave at the first sign of trouble. Their walk with God is more a relationship of convenience, and their commitment to the church is loose at best. They have never understood the covenant!

In 1 Corinthians 11:25 Paul quoted Jesus' words that this is a "new covenant in My blood." The relationship Jesus offers is permanent. It is all-inclusive.

#1 answer: c

It is real. When we enter a relationship with Him, we can count on it: He will be faithful to the end. Not only will He stick it out, but He will also invest Himself in us and make us the best we can possibly be. No matter what we do, His love is true; and He will lay down His life for us.

(2) **Read Romans 8:35,37-39 in the margin and underline all the things that cannot separate us from the love of Christ.**

Romans 8:35,37-39
"Who can separate us from the love of Christ? Can affliction or anguish or persecution or famine or nakedness or danger or sword? … No, in all these things we are more than victorious through Him who loved us. For I am persuaded that neither death nor life, nor angels nor rulers, nor things present, nor things to come, nor powers, nor height, nor depth, nor any other created thing will have the power to separate us from the love of God that is in Christ Jesus our Lord!"

The cross will forever be a symbol of God's covenant relationship, for in the cross He said His love has no end. Whatever it takes, He will be faithful. We are a covenant people. When we are born again, we enter a covenant relationship with God. When we then enter the family of God, we do not merely join a church. We enter a covenant relationship with God's people.

This covenant should influence our behavior in the church. It should affect the use of our tongue when we talk about fellow church members. Our financial support of the church reflects that covenant. We serve in the church because we are committed to building up the body. And our prayer lives take on new meaning in the context of the church.

When someone becomes a member of our church, we say something like this: "Acknowledging that God has added this person to the body, will you enter a covenant with her to pray for her, to walk alongside her, and to help her become everything God desires for her life?"

The congregation responds with a hearty "Amen!" That public statement is more than a ritual; it is real. We stand together, for we are members of the same body. We celebrate with those who are saved, baptized, and dedicated. We respond to those who are in need physically, emotionally, and spiritually. We encourage those who commit their lives to God. We do whatever it takes to build up the body of Christ because we are in covenant.

Conclude today's lesson by talking with God about the covenant. Spend time with the Lord and ask Him to show you whether you are taking seriously the covenant with Him and His people. Are there ways you need to renew your commitment and remain faithful to the body to which God added you?

Day 3 • Symbols of the Covenant

Read and meditate on "God's Word for Today" and "Today's Spiritual Reality" in the margin. Begin today's study with prayer.

The covenant God has established with His people is so significant that He left His church several wonderful symbols for remembering, teaching, and even returning to the covenant on a regular basis. Our tendency to drift away (see Hebrews 2:1) is all the more reason to remember the covenant often with earnest hearts.

The Lord's Supper. When the church gathers to observe the Lord's Supper, or Communion, it is remembering the covenant. As Christians, we are in a new covenant, sealed with the blood of Christ; and the Lord's Supper recalls or renews that covenant (see 1 Corinthians 11:25). This is why the apostle Paul urged us to examine ourselves (see 1 Corinthians 11:28) before participating. A broken relationship with Christ is tantamount to a broken covenant with God. A holy God will not bless a people who have broken the new covenant, knowing that it cost Jesus His life. Communion is our opportunity to examine our relationship with Christ and to be restored to the blessings of a covenant relationship.

1. **Think about the last time you participated in the Lord's Supper. Was this more a time of ritual for you or a time to renew the covenant? Explain.**

___

___

___

Baptism. When people repent of their sin and make Christ the Lord of their lives, the first step of obedience is the ordinance of baptism. Baptism was a part of God's plan, allowing all believers to acknowledge publicly what Christ did for them. Just as Christ identified with sinful humanity through His baptism, we now identify with Christ through the same ordinance (see Romans 6:4-5). In that moment we acknowledge before a watching world that we willingly enter the new covenant in Christ.

God's Word for Today

"We must therefore pay even more attention to what we have heard, so that we will not drift away." Hebrews 2:1

Today's Spiritual Reality

We must remember the covenant.

1 Corinthians 11:25

"In the same way He also took the cup, after supper, and said, 'This cup is the new covenant in My blood. Do this, as often as you drink it, in remembrance of Me.' "

Romans 6:4-5

"We were buried with Him by baptism into death, in order that, just as Christ was raised from the dead by the glory of the Father, so we too may walk in a new way of life. For if we have been joined with Him in the likeness of His death, we will certainly also be in the likeness of His resurrection."

Baptism is a time to remember the covenant because it pictures the gospel story. It declares the death, burial, and resurrection of Christ as a person is buried under the water and rises again. Believers who are baptized declare that they have chosen to enter the new covenant and be a part of the people of God. Christians who observe baptism can recall the decision they made and reflect on their relationship with Christ.

(2) **Have you obeyed the Lord and professed your faith through baptism?**
○ Yes ○ No

(3) **Why is baptism done publicly before a congregation? Check all that apply.**
○ a. First step of obedience to Christ
○ b. Testimony to others of entering a new life in Christ
○ c. Symbolizes entering the new covenant in Christ

#3 answers: a, b, c

Receiving members. Another time a church remembers the covenant is when the Lord adds new members to the body. The way we receive them is the way we receive Him (see John 13:20). Therefore, we treat new members as a gift from God and commit ourselves to being part of His great plan of salvation. The entire congregation welcomes the person into the covenant relationship. For the new member, it is much more than joining a church. It is entering a covenant with fellow believers who seek to follow Christ. For the church, it is reaffirming the covenant relationship and the commitment to join Christ in the work of the kingdom.

John 13:20
"I assure you: The one who receives whomever I send receives Me, and the one who receives Me receives Him who sent Me."

Many churches also offer a new-member class, which helps orient people to the expectations of people in the covenant. It helps people grow in their walk with God and challenges them to do their part to build up the body.

(4) **List in the margin the three opportunities for a church to remember the covenant.**

Opportunities for a Church to Remember the Covenant

1. ____________________
2. ____________________
3. ____________________

The next time you see one of these events in the life of your church, remember the covenant you made with God and His people. Remember them often so that you will not drift from the blessing of a covenant relationship.

Conclude today's lesson by talking with God about the covenant relationship you have with Him. Thank Him for the cross, for your baptism, and for adding you to Christ's body.

Day 4 • Testing the Covenant

God's Word for Today

"Stand firm in one spirit, with one mind, working side by side for the faith of the gospel." Philippians 1:27

Today's Spiritual Reality

Crisis is an opportunity to display the covenant and to reflect the love of God.

Read and meditate on "God's Word for Today" and "Today's Spiritual Reality" in the margin. Begin today's study with prayer.

One benefit of a covenant is evident when a church goes through crises. In these moments a covenant is needed the most.

1. **When a crisis comes in your church, what is your first reaction?**
   - ○ a. Ask God to use me to help in any way possible
   - ○ b. Look for others to get us out of the situation
   - ○ c. Blame others and complain about the problem
   - ○ d. Run away from the problem and join another church
   - ○ e. Other: ______________________________

When your church faces trouble, what should you do? Go to a more healthy church? Criticize the pastor or leadership? Or perhaps quietly back away and let others deal with the problem? None of those responses are appropriate for a church member. Because you are in a covenant relationship, you will stand with them and intercede on their behalf. Romans 12:5 states, "We who are many are one body in Christ and individually members of one another." We are connected to one another in the body of Christ. Whether times are good or trying, we must walk together before God.

We are connected to one another in the body of Christ. Whether times are good or trying, we must walk together before God.

Every church goes through a crisis from time to time. It happened in our church during a building project. While we were building a new sanctuary, a mechanical engineer made a mistake on the heating and air-conditioning system; and the revised plan doubled the cost of that component. At a called business meeting, our building committee reported cost overruns, significant financial need, and the challenge to finish the building. Even worse, the bank that had given us a line of credit to finish the building got nervous and threatened to shut down the project!

I remember the packed room and nervous looks on the faces of our leaders. What would the congregation say? How would they respond? An older man stood up and said, "I have made mistakes in the past and am sure to make some in the future. But I want our leaders to know that we are proud of them and are glad to have them leading our church." Then he began to clap his hands with encouragement. Instantly, the entire congregation rose to their feet and gave the leaders a standing ovation.

Tears began to well up in the eyes of those who had just delivered bad news, for the congregation communicated, "You are not alone. We stand together. We are family." I witnessed what a healthy relationship in the family of God looks like in which people love one another and work out their struggles together. And I think the Father smiled!

The greatest concern on God's heart is that we have a love relationship with the family—a love relationship with Him and a love relationship with one another. In fact, walking in a love relationship with other believers through difficult times is the clearest evidence that you are in fact a Christian: "We know that we have passed from death to life because we love our brothers. The one who does not love remains in death" (1 John 3:14).

Walking in a love relationship with other believers through difficult times is the clearest evidence that you are in fact a Christian.

That is what a covenant is meant to do. It is a trust relationship between God's people that allows them to work through any crisis. In fact, God allows times of crisis so that we can see where we stand with one another—so that we can test the covenant and see where our commitments lie.

(2) **Read Daniel 9:4-7 in the margin and circle the words *we* and *us*.**

Daniel 9:4-7
"I prayed to the LORD my God and confessed: Ah, Lord—the great and awe-inspiring God who keeps His gracious covenant with those who love Him and keep His commandments—we have sinned, done wrong, acted wickedly, rebelled, and turned away from Your commandments and ordinances. We have not listened to Your servants the prophets, who spoke in Your name to our kings, leaders, fathers, and all the people of the land. Lord, righteousness belongs to You, but this day public shame belongs to us."

Daniel obviously understood what it meant to be in covenant with God and His people. As the most righteous man in the nation, Daniel had not personally committed the sins mentioned in his prayer. But as far as he was concerned, if the nation had sinned, he was standing with them. He was not going to abandon them in a dark time but plead the case on their behalf. Because of his righteousness God heard him. That is what walking together in covenant looks like—the strong helping the weak, the mature helping the immature, the godly encouraging the sinner. We are in this life together.

Conclude today's lesson by talking with God about your church family. If you are currently facing a crisis, ask the Lord how He wants you to respond. If you've been through a crisis and did not respond as God would have desired, seek His forgiveness. Pray that the Lord will prepare your church to walk in loving relationship with one another when troubled times come.

Day 5 • Blessing in the Covenant

God's Word for Today

"Just as each of us has one body with many members, and these members do not all have the same function, so in Christ we who are many form one body, and each member belongs to all the others."
Romans 12:4-5, NIV

Today's Spiritual Reality

In the covenant relationship of the church, we belong to one another; we need one another.

Read and meditate on "God's Word for Today" and "Today's Spiritual Reality" in the margin. Begin today's study with prayer.

This week you have processed a lot of information about fellowship with believers, and you have been challenged to respond along the way. Here is your next challenge: are you ready and willing to live according to God's design for a covenant relationship in the body of Christ and in your local church?

1. **Turn to page 25 and read the list of possible responses to this week's study. Choose one of these suggestions or identify something else you can and will do to show your commitment to a covenant relationship with your brothers and sisters in Christ in your church.**

____

____

Remember that salvation is extremely personal, but it is not private. The context of God's salvation is always His larger purposes for His people. Your personal relationship with God always affects the people of God among whom you have been placed. God has made His body personally and collectively interdependent.

God has made His body personally and collectively interdependent.

Even in the old covenant God made with the nation of Israel, He gave instructions that were to guide them in their relationship with Him and His people. The Ten Commandments gave instruction on both relationships. The nation affected every individual, and every individual affected the nation. In the New Testament this relationship among Christians in the early church also demonstrates an interdependent relationship. Individuals who entered a saving relationship with Christ also entered a vital relationship with God's people in a local church.

God has graciously offered to sinful humanity an intimate relationship with Himself. God has never forced and will never force spiritual possessions on us; He gives us the choice whether to receive them. Yet we must respond to His offer and enter the covenant relationship with Him. When you were born again, you entered the covenant with God and His people.

So how do we experience the full blessings of this covenant? How do we live in a covenant relationship with God and experience the purpose of our creation? Wholeheartedly. The first and greatest commandment is "Love the Lord your God with all your heart, with all your soul, and with all your mind" (Matthew 22:37). The covenant requires wholehearted love. It cannot be any other way; the way we respond to God reflects our belief in Him.

Within the covenant someone who gives less than his whole heart will receive much less than what he could have experienced in his relationship with God. The person who holds back from loving the church will miss out on most of what God wanted to do in his life, for God promises and gives in the same measure that we are ready to step out in faith and give to Him and His people. If your love for the people of God were the measure God used for blessing your life, how full would your life be?

2 Read Luke 6:38 in the margin and answer the following questions.

a. How does God treat those who give generously? ________________

____

b. What is the standard God uses to measure His blessing in your life?

____

I wonder whether the reason many Christians experience little blessing is that they entered a relationship with God with little faith. Because their walk with God is halfhearted, they do not experience the promises of God in all their fullness. Are they reaping what they have sown?

Talk to God about your desire to trust Him and live in covenant relationship with Him and His people with wholehearted love. Ask Him to make clear to you the specific steps you can take to live that reality.

Review this week's lessons and underline the statement or Scripture God seemed to emphasize to you the most. Ask the Lord to show you how He wants you to respond to Him and to His people in light of what He has said to you this week. Write in the margin a prayer of response to the Lord.

Luke 6:38
"Give, and it will be given to you; a good measure—pressed down, shaken together, and running over—will be poured into your lap. For with the measure you use, it will be measured back to you."

Responding to the Lord

Session 2 • The Covenant

Use some or all of the following suggestions to guide your small-group experience this week.

Opening Prayer

Building Relationships

1. When and how did you decide to become a part of this church family?
2. What is one way another member of your church has been a blessing to you or has inspired you live and act more like Christ?

Responding to Learning Activities

Share your responses to some or all of the following learning activities.

- Page 27, activity 3
- Page 30, activity 1
- Page 32, activity 1. How should a believer respond?
- Page 34, activity 1

Reviewing Week 2

1. In pairs or triads take turns reciting your Scripture-memory verses, Hebrews 10:24-25.
2. Review this week's daily spiritual realities, reproduced below. Which one do you think identifies a reality you and your church most need to develop more fully so that you will experience God's best as a fellowship of believers? Why?
   - Day 1: We are members of the body of Christ.
   - Day 2: Fellowship in the church is based on a trust relationship.
   - Day 3: We must remember the covenant.
   - Day 4: Crisis is an opportunity to display the covenant and to reflect the love of God.
   - Day 5: In the covenant relationship of the church, we belong to one another; we need one another.
3. Why is our understanding of membership so important for our church?
4. In your own words, define the word *covenant* and explain how it impacts your relationship with God and your church (day 2).

5. What are three opportunities for a church to remember the covenant? Why is each an important time for you and your church (day 3)?
6. How should we react when the Lord allows our church to experience crisis (day 4)?
7. How did Daniel illustrate his commitment to a covenant with God's people in his prayer in Daniel 9 (p. 33)?
8. Why is it so important for each member to accept and live according to the covenant with God and His people?

Building Up the Body

1. During your review at the end of day 5, what statement or Scripture did you identify that you think God emphasized most this week?
2. Which truth that you have studied this week do you think would do the most to build up the body of Christ if you and other members of your church faithfully applied it?
3. How do you want to respond to what you have learned this week? How has the Lord prompted you this week to love His people and build up His body?

Praying Together

Volunteers, pray in the following ways.

1. Thank God for His covenant and for the people with whom He has placed you in covenant.
2. Ask God to help you grow in oneness with one another and with Him.
3. Ask God to guide your church to live in relationship with one another as He desires, especially in times of crisis.

Preview Week 3

Turn to page 39 and preview the study for the coming week.

Week 3

The Body of Christ

"As we have many parts in one body, and all the parts do not have the same function, in the same way we who are many are one body in Christ and individually members of one another."

Romans 12:4-5

The Body of Christ

OVERVIEW OF WEEK 3

Day 1: Members Connected in Christ
Day 2: God Adds to the Body
Day 3: Interdependence
Day 4: Building Up the Body
Day 5: Directed by Christ, the Head

VERSES TO MEMORIZE

"As we have many parts in one body, and all the parts do not have the same function, in the same way we who are many are one body in Christ and individually members of one another" (Romans 12:4-5).

DISCIPLESHIP HELPS FOR WEEK 3

"My Place in His Body" (p. 97)
"Instructions for the Body of Christ in Romans 12:9-21" (pp. 98–99)

POSSIBLE RESPONSES TO WEEK 3

As I discover the way the church is to function as the body of Christ, I will respond by doing things like the following.

- I will seek to be more connected with people in my church family.
- I will try to get to know people the Lord has recently added to my church.
- I will pray for and encourage the leaders God has placed in our body to equip the members for acts of ministry to build up the body.
- I will receive training so that I'll be able to help build up the body through acts of ministry.
- I will find my place of service to others in the body of Christ and receive ministry from others as an interdependent member of the body.
- I will look for ways to build up the body by showing Christ's love to people in my church who have needs.
- I will pray with my church family when we gather for prayer.

God's Word for Today
"You are the body of Christ, and individual members of it."
1 Corinthians 12:27

Today's Spiritual Reality
We are connected together in Christ to form His body.

Day 1 • Members Connected in Christ

Read and meditate on "God's Word for Today" and "Today's Spiritual Reality" in the margin. Begin today's study with prayer.

Many people equate church membership with club membership. This view could not be further from the truth. As the church, we don't constitute a club but the living body of Christ.

Our connection with other church members is deep and secure. When Christ redeemed us, the Heavenly Father caused us to be born again into His family. We are His children, along with many spiritual brothers and sisters. We are linked in Christ with these spiritual siblings for all eternity. God's purpose is for us to reflect this connection here on earth as we join our lives with Him and one another to form His body, the church.

1. **Mark the following statements *T* for *true* or *F* for *false*.**
   ___ 1. A church is the living body of Christ, not just another organization.
   ___ 2. We are linked in Christ with many spiritual siblings.
   ___ 3. God joins us together in Christ to form His body.

Often we refer to our local church as our church body. This term is not wrong; but ultimately, our church is the body of Christ. We are not simply a group of believers who come together with common interests. Our church is the living body of Christ (see 1 Corinthians 12:27).

1 Corinthians 12:27
"You are the body of Christ."

Viewing each church member as a member of Christ's body is crucial in determining whether we will truly function as His body. The way we treat one another reveals whether we understand this truth. Those who understand seek to build up and care for Christ's body by loving and encouraging the people of God. Those who don't understand feel free to criticize or hurt another member of the church, apparently not realizing they are hurting Christ Himself.

2. **When you hurt other members of Christ's body, how are you treating Christ? Check one.**
   ○ a. This has nothing to do with Christ.
   ○ b. I cause Him to hurt because I've wounded a member of His body.

#1 answers: 1-T, 2-T, 3-T

As individuals, we may want to focus exclusively on our own personal connection and relationship with the Lord. We may want to experience the personal fullness of Jesus' words "Remain in Me, and I in you" (John 15:4). However, we cannot personally experience all of our relationship with Christ if we are not connected to His people, the body of Christ.

Paul pointed to this connection in Romans 12:4-5. In verse 5 he stated, "In the same way we who are many are one body in Christ and individually members of one another." Not only are we members of Christ, but we are also members of one another in Christ. When we recognize this truth, we will seek to care for one another and build up one another. Our love for Christ compels us to care for His body. At this point we truly begin to function together as the body of Christ.

When we realize that we are spiritually connected to one another in Christ, we will begin to know how to function as Christ's body. We will understand the meaning of 1 Corinthians 12:26: "If one member suffers, all the members suffer with it; if one member is honored, all the members rejoice with it." What happens to one happens to all because we are connected in Christ.

Our relationship with Christ will be incomplete as long as we attempt to live independently of His body. He wants us to be connected to Him and one another. Without this connection we will never know the fullness of our love relationship with Him or the joy of having Him accomplish His purpose through us. Only together "with all the saints" (Ephesians 3:18) can we experience the full dimensions of Christ's love.

3. Based on Paul's prayer in Ephesians 3:17-19, how can you best experience the breadth, width, height, and depth of Christ's (the Messiah's) love? Check one.

○ a. When I'm all alone with Him in a private place
○ b. When I'm firmly established in a love relationship Him together with "all the saints.

Conclude today's lesson by talking with God about your connection to the rest of the body of Christ. Use Paul's prayer in Ephesians 3:17-19 as a prayer for your church. Ask the Lord to help you become someone who cares for His body. Express to the Lord your desire to be deeply connected to Him and those in His body.

#2 answer: b

We cannot personally experience all of our relationship with Christ if we are not connected to His people, the body of Christ.

Ephesians 3:17-19
"I pray that you, being rooted and firmly established in love, may be able to comprehend with all the saints what is the breadth and width, height and depth, and to know the Messiah's love that surpasses knowledge, so you may be filled with all the fullness of God."

Day 2 • God Adds to the Body

Read and meditate on "God's Word for Today" and "Today's Spiritual Reality" in the margin. Begin today's study with prayer.

It's easy to look at a vibrant church and credit the pastor or the congregation with the church's growth. But if the church is really vibrant from God's perspective, He is the only one who deserves credit. Sure, He will work through us as we follow Him; but it is He, not we, who will build His body.

1. Read Matthew 16:18 in the margin and circle the name of the one who builds the church of Christ.

God has a plan He desires to accomplish through your church. Then He shapes your church according to this plan. His plan may call for your church to be small, medium, or large. A church's size doesn't determine health. A healthy church is one that is built by God and is walking in His purposes.

2. Select the word or statement that describes a healthy church.

○ a. Large
○ b. Small
○ c. Built by God for His purposes
○ d. Medium

In our Christian culture, church leaders are pressured to have a numerically growing church. Obviously, reaching people is very important, but we sometimes make great efforts to attract people to our church. We may select a good church-growth plan and begin to implement it. Having a good strategy is not bad, but the danger lies in trying to build our church instead of asking God to shape His body for His purpose.

Many Christians choose a church based on its health—the activities that can benefit their lives and families. This is a self-centered approach. If Christ is truly our Lord, we will seek to discover where He wants to place us. Surprising to some, He may even choose to send us to an unhealthy church and use us to help bring it back to health. Wherever He chooses to send us, we must then ask Him to use us to build up His body.

God does not haphazardly bring someone into His body. When God leads someone to join your church, He performs a very deliberate act.

God's Word for Today
"God has placed the parts, each one of them, in the body just as He wanted."
1 Corinthians 12:18

Today's Spiritual Reality
God is the one who adds members to your church body.

Matthew 16:18
"I [Jesus] will build My church, and the forces of Hades will not overpower it."

A healthy church is one that is built by God and is walking in His purposes.

#2 answer: c

He strategically places the person within the body to accomplish His purpose through your church. Intentionally get to know them and take seriously the fact that God has added them to His body.

3 How did you decide to be part of the church to which you currently belong? Write a brief explanation in the margin.

Be careful not to place levels of importance on church members. Viewing certain members as more important than others is not biblical. First Corinthians 12:18 says that God has "placed the parts, each one of them, in the body just as He wanted." He has designed each of us uniquely for His purpose. Therefore, He places each person in His body with an important function. Without that member His body would not function as He desires.

A few years ago the Lord brought a man named Arly to our church. Arly, in his mid-80s, had recently lost his wife. The Lord had made it very clear that He wanted Arly to move to our town. When we heard the details of Arly's amazing testimony, it became clear that God was adding him to our church. Arly knew he couldn't do all the things he had once done, but he wanted to be faithful to his Lord. It has been amazing to watch the way the Lord has used Arly to build up the body. He always encourages others and is a powerful example of faithfulness. Anyone who spends time with him always comes away desiring to follow the Lord more earnestly. Without Arly our church would not be what God intended.

Identify one person in your church who has encouraged you to follow Christ more faithfully. Thank God for adding that person to your church family.

In God's wisdom He places each member in His body. It wasn't by chance that He added you to your church. However, if you refuse to function as the Lord intends, His body will not function as it should.

If you refuse to function as the Lord intends, His body will not function as it should.

4 Will you allow God to work through you to build up His body and glorify His name? ○ Yes ○ No

Conclude today's lesson by talking with God about ways He may want you to serve in the body. How does Jesus want to work through you to build up His body? Ask Him.

Day 3 • Interdependence

God's Word for Today
"The body is not one part, but many."
1 Corinthians 12:14

Today's Spiritual Reality
As members of Christ's body, we are interdependent.

Read and meditate on "God's Word for Today" and "Today's Spiritual Reality" in the margin. Begin today's study with prayer.

The way God made the human body is fascinating. Each part plays a vital role in the body's functioning as God designed. If one part stops functioning, the whole body knows it and focuses on fixing the problem. Our body parts are interdependent. God designed the human body to function as one unit with many parts. Each part depends on all the other parts.

The body of Christ is designed to function the same way. Members of the body of Christ are interdependent; they are mutually dependent on one another and mutually beneficial to one another. We need one another. For the body to be healthy, all members of the body must function where the Lord placed them. Understanding interdependence is crucial for a church to function as the body of Christ.

1 Corinthians 12:19
"If they were all the same part, where would the body be?"

It's astounding to look at the uniqueness of the people God brings together in a church to form His body. He intentionally puts people together whom He has shaped differently. Difference is good (see 1 Corinthians 12:19). His purpose is not for members of the body to be in conflict but to work together and complement one another. This happens when members realize that God created them to be interdependent.

We can see how interdependence functions when a church obediently accepts an assignment it cannot complete alone. In our church the busiest week of the year is when we conduct Vacation Bible School. This week requires dozens of workers to minister to the children. We're amazed to see how God pulls this unique group of workers together. Some are great with children, while others are good at administration. He calls extroverts to work alongside introverts. As they work together in interdependence, the Lord accomplishes His will.

As they work together in interdependence, the Lord accomplishes His will.

Briefly describe a time when your church came together as one to accomplish an assignment from the Lord.

____

____

Another time interdependence is displayed in our church is when a member hurts. During crises we realize how much we need one another. Jesus told us that life will have its share of trouble (see John 16:33). This is one reason He joins us together with other believers. When trouble comes, we can minister to one another and help carry one another's burdens. Without interdependence in the body of Christ, we would go through these times alone.

John 16:33
"I have told you these things so that in Me you may have peace. You will have suffering in this world. Be courageous! I have conquered the world."

The early church seemed to understand that it was to live in this type of interdependent relationship. When God called believers to share the gospel, they did it together. The end of Acts 2 records that the Lord brought people to salvation as this group was "continuing daily with one accord" (Acts 2:46, NKJV). They worked together as one body to obey God's assignment.

When trouble comes, we can minister to one another and help carry one another's burdens.

It is also interesting to see how the early church approached times of trouble. As in any congregation, some believers experienced difficulty. Luke continually pointed out in Acts that the church responded by doing whatever was necessary to meet the need. Because members were interdependent, they knew their job was to walk with one another, especially during times of need.

Interdependence was not optional for the early church, and it is not optional for us today. God designed us to work together as His body. We do this by living in a mutually dependent relationship with one another.

2. **Paul gives specific instructions for the way members of the body of Christ are to live in relationship with one another. Turn to pages 98–99 and complete "Instructions for the Body of Christ in Romans 12:9-21." Then write below one action you sense God wants you to take immediately about your role in your church as an interdependent member.**

____

____

Conclude today's lesson by talking with God about the way He has built your church with many members who are different. Reflect on those who have played parts in your spiritual life and thank God for them. Ask the Lord to mold you into someone who helps others in times of need. Do specific people come to mind who need ministry or service from you? If God brings a person or an action to mind, write a note to yourself in the margin.

Day 4 • Building Up the Body

Read and meditate on "God's Word for Today" and "Today's Spiritual Reality" in the margin. Begin today's study with prayer.

God has given us the assignment to build up His body. He placed each of us in the church family He determined was best for His kingdom. Now He wants to work through us to build it up. The way we function as a member of Christ's body will determine whether we build it up or tear it down. Whether or not we realize it, our lives do one or the other.

1. **If you had to evaluate your contribution to (a) building up or (b) tearing down the body of Christ, which be most accurate? Circle one.**

Did you want a third option, "(c) I don't do either"? We can tear down the body of Christ in two ways. First, we can refuse to function the way God purposed. In the human body, if the eyes refuse to function as they should, the whole body is adversely affected. The body of Christ functions the same way. If you, as one part of the body, do not function as God intended, the whole body suffers.

Second, we tear down the body when we do not actively love God's people. To love like Jesus means we place others above ourselves. Today many church members refuse to do this. Instead, we try to make sure our personal rights are always honored. If we feel our rights are dishonored, we take out our anger on another member. The results are pain and division within the body. Relating to fellow members in an unloving manner damages the body of Christ.

2. **Complete each sentence by matching the beginning on the left with the correct ending on the right.**

___ 1. Refusing to love God's people … a. builds up the body.
___ 2. Seeking to love God's people … b. tears down the body.

Someone who is being transformed by the love of Christ will want to build up His body. In 2 Corinthians 5 Paul stated that the Holy Spirit would help the Corinthians comprehend the love of Christ. Then they would be moved (compelled) to "no longer live for themselves, but for the One who

God's Word for Today

"He personally gave some to be apostles, some prophets, some evangelists, some pastors and teachers, for the training of the saints in the work of ministry, to build up the body of Christ." Ephesians 4:11-12

Today's Spiritual Reality

God intends for us to build up His body.

2 Corinthians 5:14-15

"Christ's love compels us, since we have reached this conclusion: if One died for all, then all died. And He died for all so that those who live should no longer live for themselves, but for the One who died for them and was raised."

#2 answers: 1-b, 2-a

died for them and was raised" (2 Corinthians 5:15). He also knew this would dramatically affect how they related to one another.

When we live for Christ, the only thing that really matters is knowing what is on His heart so that we can adjust our lives and obey Him. Obedience ceases to be an obligation but the passion of our hearts. Knowing that the Lord has uniquely shaped us to function within His body, we seek to obey Him and to function as He desires. As we do, His body is built up.

The important thing is not what part we play in the body but whether we seek to be faithful to our Lord. One person may be a teacher, while another performs administrative duties. As each is faithful to the Lord, the whole body is built up. Faithfully functioning in the body as the Lord desires always builds up the body (see Ephesians 4:15-16).

We also build up the body by seeking to love one another in any way possible. Love is the foundational element in the way God works through us to build up His body.

3 **Which statement most accurately characterizes your church?**
- ○ a. The body is being built up as members serve and love one another.
- ○ b. The body is being built up to a certain degree but not fully.
- ○ c. My church is being torn down by bickering and selfishness.
- ○ d. Other: ____

____

We are to fulfill our function within the body in love. There are many ways God wants us to love His people, so look for ways the Lord might want you to show His love to others. When a church takes seriously Jesus' command to love one another, Christ's body is built up.

4 **Turn to page 97 and read the article "My Place in His Body." Then follow the prayer suggestion at the end of the article.**

Conclude today's lesson by talking with God about ways you can contribute to building up the body of Christ. Slowly read Ephesians 3:14-19 in your Bible as a prayer for yourself and for those in your church family.

Knowing that the Lord has uniquely shaped us to function within His body, we seek to obey Him and to function as He desires. As we do, His body is built up.

Ephesians 4:15-16
"Let us grow in every way into Him who is the head—Christ. From Him the whole body, fitted and knit together by every supporting ligament, promotes the growth of the body for building up itself in love by the proper working of each individual part."

Day 5 • Directed by Christ, the Head

God's Word for Today
"'He put everything under His feet' and appointed Him as head over everything for the church, which is His body." Ephesians 1:22-23

Today's Spiritual Reality
Christ, as the head, directs His body as He desires.

Read and meditate on "God's Word for Today" and "Today's Spiritual Reality" in the margin. Begin today's study with prayer.

When God adds us to a local body, we need to learn from the Lord how He intends for us to function. It is important to know whether we are to function as a hand instead of an ear! So we need to take time and ask God to show us how He is working in our church and how He intends for us to function. God's place for each of us may change over time or perhaps as He moves us from place to place. However, the role of head of the body belongs solely to Christ. He alone is the one who directs His body.

1. **To whom has God given the role of head of the body? Check one.**
   - ○ a. Me
   - ○ b. Christ alone
   - ○ c. The pastor
   - ○ d. Deacons and elders

#1 answer: b

Christ's headship of the church mirrors the role He plays in our individual lives. Christ is to be not only our Savior but also our Lord. As His disciples, we get our direction from Him. If we refuse to follow Him as Lord, our walk with Him comes to a grinding stop. The same holds true for a church. If we refuse to allow Christ to function as the head of our church, we cease to function effectively as His body.

Matthew 7:21
"Not everyone who says to Me, 'Lord, Lord!' will enter the kingdom of heaven, but only the one who does the will of My Father in heaven."

Unfortunately, many Christians have not taken seriously the fact that Christ is the Lord of their lives. The result is that they neither seek to know what He desires nor follow Him (see Matthew 7:21). This affects the way our church functions. If we do not allow Him to direct our lives, we will not know how He intends to direct our church.

1 Corinthians 2:12
"We have not received the spirit of the world, but the Spirit who is from God, in order to know what has been freely given to us by God."

Christ is not a figurehead; He is the head. If He is to function as the head of our church, we must recognize Him as such by placing all our faith in Him to communicate with us what He desires. He has given us the gift of His Spirit, who will communicate to us what is on His heart (see 1 Corinthians 2:12). As He does this, we need to make the adjustments needed to follow Him in obedience. If Christ is truly the head of our church, the most important thing we can do is to seek to know what He desires.

2. **Which best describes you and your church?**
   - ○ a. Seeking to obey and follow Christ as the Lord and head
   - ○ b. Using human reasoning to do things we think will please the Lord but not following Him as the head
   - ○ c. Other: ______________________________

The first church took corporate prayer very seriously. During these times together they sought to know what was on Christ's heart and how they were to follow Him. The Lord moved powerfully to enable and direct the early church (see Acts 4:31). He did this in direct response to the body's crying out together in prayer. We must be a church that cries out to God together in prayer. Church members must also be ready to share with others what they see God doing and hear God saying.

Acts 4:31
"When they had prayed, the place where they were assembled was shaken, and they were all filled with the Holy Spirit and began to speak God's message with boldness."

3. **Which words best describe the prayer life of your church?**

○ a. Vibrant	○ b. Nonexistent	○ c. Unimportant
○ d. Central	○ e. Vital	○ f. Ignored

Read Isaiah 56:7 in the margin. Ask the Lord to make you a person of prayer and your church a house of prayer for the nations.

Isaiah 56:7
"My house will be called a house of prayer for all nations."

Some believe the Lord guides us only into easy assignments. Remember that we are His body, and He has always been willing for His body to suffer to accomplish His Father's purpose. Experiencing Him as He accomplishes His will always brings joy. But we must never forget that the Lord will not spare our going through difficulty and pain in order to accomplish His will.

At times Christ will bring strains to His body in order to strengthen it. A difficult time in the church is an opportunity to grow and learn more fully how to follow Christ as the head. Don't assume that every difficulty is the result of sin or the enemy. God may well be the one who has brought you into that difficult place so that He can strengthen and grow His body.

Responding to the Lord

Review this week's lessons and underline the statement or Scripture God seemed to emphasize to you the most. Ask the Lord to show you how He wants you to respond to Him and to His people in light of what He has said to you this week. Write in the margin a prayer of response to the Lord.

Session 3 • The Body of Christ

Use some or all of the following suggestions to guide your small-group experience this week.

Opening Prayer

Building Relationships

Share *one* of the following with your group.

1. What has been one of your most meaningful places and experiences of service in the body of Christ? Why?
2. Describe one time when you have seen church members care for one another by giving or receiving the benefits of being the body of Christ.
3. Describe a time when you needed the help of the body of Christ but failed to receive the help you needed. Did the body know about the need? How could they have responded?

Responding to Learning Activities

Share your responses to some or all of the following learning activities.

- Page 43, activity 3
- Page 44, activity 1
- Page 98, activity 2. Identify your top two or three for the church.
- Page 45, activity 2
- Page 47, activity 3. Why?

Reviewing Week 3

1. In pairs or triads take turns reciting your Scripture-memory verses, Romans 12:4-5.
2. Review this week's daily spiritual realities, reproduced below. Which one do you think identifies a reality you and your church most need to develop more fully so that you will experience God's best as a fellowship of believers? Why?
   - Day 1: We are connected together in Christ to form His body.
   - Day 2: God is the one who adds members to your church body.
   - Day 3: As members of Christ's body, we are interdependent.
   - Day 4: God intends for us to build up His body.
   - Day 5: Christ, as the head, directs His body as He desires.
3. How would you describe what the body of Christ is and how it should function?

4. What is the connection between the way you treat other members of the body of Christ and the way you treat Christ? How should we treat those in our church family (day 1)?
5. How can you best experience the breadth, width, height, and depth of Christ's love (p. 41, activity 3)?
6. How would you describe the interdependence of members of the body of Christ (day 3)?
7. Who is the head of the church? Who are people and groups who are not the head? How can the whole church body function in such a way that the true head of the body is permitted to function that way (day 5)?
8. Why do churches often struggle to follow Christ as their head?
9. Why is corporate prayer such an important part of functioning as the body of Christ? How well do you think your church is doing (day 5 and p. 49, activities 2 and 3)?

Building Up the Body

1. During your review at the end of day 5, what statement or Scripture did you identify that you think God emphasized most this week?
2. Which truth that you have studied this week do you think would do the most to build up the body of Christ if you and other members of your church faithfully applied it?
3. How do you want to respond to what you have learned this week? How has the Lord prompted you this week to love His people and build up His body?
4. Describe a time when you saw a church come together to accomplish an assignment from the Lord.
5. Do you sense that God is guiding your church to an assignment you must accomplish together? Explain.

Praying Together

Take turns praying brief prayers for yourselves and for your church to function as the body of Christ in ways that please and honor Him. Ask God to guide your prayers, based on what you have discussed today.

Preview Week 4

Turn to page 53 and preview the study for the coming week.

Week 4

Koinonia: God's Love Expressed

"If we walk in the light
as He Himself is in the light,
we have fellowship with
one another, and the blood
of Jesus His Son cleanses
us from all sin."

1 John 1:7

Koinonia: *God's Love Expressed*

OVERVIEW OF WEEK 4

Day 1: Fellowship with God
Day 2: Fellowship with One Another
Day 3: Fellowship in Its Fullness
Day 4: Dangers to Avoid
Day 5: The Testimony of Fellowship

VERSE TO MEMORIZE

"If we walk in the light as He Himself is in the light, we have fellowship with one another, and the blood of Jesus His Son cleanses us from all sin" (1 John 1:7).

DISCIPLESHIP HELP FOR WEEK 4

" 'One Anothers' for the Body of Christ" (pp. 100–101)

POSSIBLE RESPONSES TO WEEK 4

As I realize the importance of healthy fellowship with God and other believers, I will respond by doing things like the following.

- I will do all God leads me to do in order to experience the fullness of *koinonia* with Him and with His people.
- I will watch for opportunities to obey the "one another" passages in the New Testament as I live a Christlike life in my relationships with other believers.
- I will urgently seek, with the Lord's help and guidance, to reconcile with anyone with whom I have a broken relationship.
- I will find ways to more freely share my relationship with the Lord with people in my church family so that we can experience true *koinonia* with God and one another.
- I will take seriously the dangers to *koinonia* that I see in my life. With God's help I will get rid of those that hinder fellowship with Him and others.
- I will make my life available to the Lord, giving Him access to express true *koinonia* in my church through me.

Day 1 • Fellowship with God

God's Word for Today
"This is eternal life, that they may know You, the only true God, and the One You have sent—Jesus Christ." John 17:3

Today's Spiritual Reality
We can have intimate fellowship with God.

Read and meditate on "God's Word for Today" and "Today's Spiritual Reality" in the margin. Begin today's study with prayer.

Most people recognize that there is a God, but few have experienced a genuine love relationship with Him. Some argue that God is unknowable to human experience. If our relationship with God were based on our human ability to know Him, their claim would be absolutely true. God would be unknowable. How can a finite creature know an infinite Creator? He can't unless the Creator makes Himself known to the creature.

The truth is that God has made Himself known, and He is active in the world today. He has revealed Himself to us in many different ways. The greatest revelation, however, is found in the person of His Son, Jesus Christ. While talking to His disciples, Jesus said He is the way to the Father, for He and the Father are one (see John 14:6-7). The reason Jesus came to earth was to provide a way we could know and experience God.

John 14:6-7
"Jesus told him, 'I am the way, the truth, and the life. No one comes to the Father except through Me. If you know Me, you will also know My Father. From now on you do know Him and have seen Him.' "

Pause for a moment and thank God for sending Jesus to show you what He is like.

We do not serve a God who watches from a distance. We serve a God who desires a love relationship with us that is real and personal. So how do we relate to God and experience a love relationship with Him? A relationship with God must be experienced in life in order for it to have value.

1. **As you read the following definition, underline the word or words that best help you understand the meaning of *koinonia* with God.**

*Koinonia** is a Greek term the New Testament writers used to describe the practical expression of God's love toward His people. Sometimes it is translated *fellowship, partnership, sharing,* or even *stewardship.* The term expresses the way God's love is manifested in real life and is the standard by which we are to love one another. *Koinonia* is the way we experience the fullness of God's love for His people and in His people. In a real sense, *koinonia* is the essence of God's great salvation. *Koinonia* is also the basis of the way we relate to one another as the family of God.

* ***koinonia:*** fellowship, partnership, sharing, stewardship, love in action

Without a personal relationship with God, there is no salvation; there is no eternal life. The relationship is not about external acts of ritual; it is an internal response of the heart. Salvation frees us from sin so that we can know God. Some people think we are freed from sin in order to act right; yet God's desire is that we *be* right. God created us to be in a right relationship with Him. "God's Word for Today," John 17:3, illustrates the significance of *koinonia,* the personal interaction between God and His people.

The first and greatest commandment is to love God with all our heart, soul, mind, and strength (see Deuteronomy 6:5; Matthew 22:37-38). Our relationship with God is to be first and foremost in our lives. As we experience a relationship with God, He expects us to relate to others in the family of God the way He relates to us.

Jesus told a parable about a servant who owed his master a great sum of money (see Matthew 18:21-35). The servant deserved to be thrown in jail, but the master was gracious and forgave the debt. Now free, the servant found a fellow servant who owed him a small amount of money and, instead of showing mercy, had him thrown in jail. When the master heard about it, he was angry. After being forgiven of a great debt, the servant was not willing to forgive a small one! The master asked the servant, "Shouldn't you also have had mercy on your fellow slave, as I had mercy on you?" (v. 33). He then revoked the gift and had the servant thrown in prison.

Deuteronomy 6:5
"Love the LORD your God with all your heart, with all your soul, and with all your strength."

Matthew 22:37-38
" 'Love the Lord your God with all your heart, with all your soul, and with all your mind.' This is the greatest and most important commandment."

(2) **Write some words below that describe God's love for you. Then compare what you wrote with the list in "God's Love" in the margin.**

____

As God blesses us in our relationship with Him, we must watch for ways we can bless those around us. To those who receive much, much is required.

(3) **Turn to " 'One Anothers' for the Body of Christ" on pages 100–101 to identify biblical instructions for living in relationship with one another in the body of Christ.**

Conclude today's lesson by talking with God about your desire to experience intimate fellowship with Him and your willingness to treat others the way He relates to you.

God's Love

- Merciful
- Gracious
- Generous
- Sacrificial
- Forgiving
- Patient
- Kind
- Never fails

Day 2 • Fellowship with One Another

God's Word for Today
"If we walk in the light as He is in the light, we have fellowship with one another, and the blood of Jesus His Son cleanses us from all sin." 1 John 1:7

Today's Spiritual Reality
God expects us to have sincere fellowship with one another.

1 John 1:6
"If we say, 'We have fellowship with Him,' and walk in darkness, we are lying and are not practicing the truth."

1 John 2:9-11
"The one who says he is in the light but hates his brother is in the darkness until now. The one who loves his brother remains in the light, and there is no cause for stumbling in him. But the one who hates his brother is in the darkness, walks in the darkness, and doesn't know where he's going, because the darkness has blinded his eyes."

#2 answer: b

Read and meditate on "God's Word for Today" and "Today's Spiritual Reality" in the margin. Begin today's study with prayer.

The word *koinonia,* which describes our relationship with God, is the same word John used in 1 John 1:3-7 to describe our relationship with the family of God. In other words, the love relationship expressed between God and His people is the same love relationship we are to share with others in the church. His love in us ought to flow through us to those in the church.

1. **Read 1 John 1:6; 2:9-11 in the margin. If we claim to be in fellowship with God yet have broken relationships and hatred toward other believers, how does the Bible describe our actions? ______________**

We're liars! Broken relationships with God's people are a symptom of a broken relationship with God. If you see people at odds with one another, what is their problem? Their primary need is to be reconciled with God, and then God will help them be reconciled with one another. So what is the best way to have fellowship in the church? Help people have fellowship with God. Then the life of God in them will affect every other relationship in their lives.

2. **What is the best way to help God's people reconcile with one another? Check one.**
   - ○ a. Put them in a room and don't let them out until they have straightened out their differences.
   - ○ b. Help them first have a vibrant fellowship *(koinonia)* with God.
   - ○ c. Take a vote and require all to agree with the majority.

Getting right with God is the first and best step to take in order to get right with others. The same is true for you. If you have broken relationships in your life, seek God with all your heart. Make sure you are right with Him. Then allow His love to fill you and enable you to love those around you.

To make your fellowship with others like your fellowship with God, first identify the ways God has reached out to you. He has forgiven you. He has been merciful to you as a sinner. He has been gracious to give you what you did not deserve. He has protected you. He has been your friend. He has expressed love in a thousand different ways. It is vital that you recognize the way God has loved you, because He commands you to love one another in the same way (see John 13:34-35). Identifying the way God loves you helps you know how to love others in His family.

An example can be cited in the area of forgiveness. God expects that we forgive others in exactly the same way He forgives us. Jesus said in the Lord's Prayer, "Forgive us our debts, as we also have forgiven our debtors" (Matthew 6:12). Look carefully at what Jesus said. If there is any doubt about what He meant by that statement, He gave a commentary on it just two verses later.

John 13:34-35
"I give you a new commandment: love one another. Just as I have loved you, you must also love one another. By this all people will know that you are My disciples, if you have love for one another."

(3) **Read Matthew 6:14-15 in the margin and answer the following.**

a. Does God forgive your sin simply because you ask Him?
○ Yes ○ No ○ I'd rather not say.

b. How does your unforgiveness of others affect your relationship with God?

____

Matthew 6:14-15
"If you forgive people their wrongdoing, your heavenly Father will forgive you as well. But if you don't forgive people, your Father will not forgive your wrongdoing."

When God's people are unwilling to forgive others, they remain unforgiven, living under the weight of their own sin. Furthermore, their growing accumulation of sin creates a barrier between them and God. They feel distant from God, and that distance brings an emptiness to their spirit.

We can plead with God all we want, but He will not forgive our sin against Him unless we are also willing to forgive those who have sinned against us. When we are in fellowship with one another, the cleansing blood of Christ covers our sin and sets us free. *Koinonia* in the family of God is vitally important because it sets you free to grow in your relationship with Almighty God. (Reread "God's Word for Today," 1 John 1:7.)

Koinonia, love in action, among members is absolutely vital to the nature of the church and to the purposes of God. This is why Christ is so concerned about our relationships with one another. His love is to be displayed and experienced within the church.

Conclude today's lesson by talking with God about your relationship with Him and how that affects your relationships with others. Is the Lord showing you someone you need to forgive? Ask Him to help you forgive him or her as Christ has forgiven you.

 # 3 answers:
a–No, I must forgive others.
b–It prevents Him from forgiving me.

Day 3 • Fellowship in Its Fullness

God's Word for Today
*"God is faithful; by Him you were called into fellowship with His Son, Jesus Christ our Lord."
1 Corinthians 1:9*

Today's Spiritual Reality
As we receive from God, we give to the people of God.

Read and meditate on "God's Word for Today" and "Today's Spiritual Reality" in the margin. Begin today's study with prayer.

Let's go a little deeper into the meaning of *koinonia*. Most people grasp the basic understanding of fellowship, but other dimensions of this word add significant meaning to our relationship with God and one another.

Partnership
1 Corinthians 3:9
"We are God's co-workers."

Partnership. What an awesome realization that we are partners with God, fellow workers in His great plan of salvation (see 1 Corinthians 3:9). Partnership is the bonding of two lives for a common purpose. Nothing is withheld in a true partnership; the resources of each one are shared with the other. Although God doesn't need us, He chooses to partner with us in the work of the gospel. Paul used this term as he talked to other believers about their partnership with him in the gospel (see Philippians 1:3-7).

Sharing
2 Peter 1:3-4
"His divine power has given us everything required for life and godliness, through the knowledge of Him who called us by His own glory and goodness. By these He has given us very great and precious promises, so that through them you may share in the divine nature, escaping the corruption that is in the world because of evil desires."

Sharing. *Koinonia* also implies sharing. It is releasing everything in you to the one with whom you are sharing. Scripture tells us that God has given us everything we need for life and godliness (see 2 Peter 1:3-4). In addition, we are told that we share in the divine nature when the Spirit of Christ comes to live in us.

Use 2 Peter 1:3-4 (in the margin) as a basis for prayer. Ask God to help you live in the reality of His divine power and nature, escaping the corruption of the world and its evil desires.

Stewardship. Another dimension of *koinonia* is stewardship. A good steward (or manager) receives not what is his but what is someone else's. Entrusted with a relationship with God, we are to be good stewards of all God has brought into our lives. We are to allow all of God's resources to flow through us to the other people of God. And God has a purpose for what He has given to us. Paul said, "Working together with Him, we also appeal to you: 'Don't receive God's grace in vain' " (2 Corinthians 6:1). That is, I do not receive all the resources of God into my life and then do nothing with them. In 1 Corinthians 15:10 Paul described his own stewardship of God's grace. *Koinonia* means we receive God's grace with a grateful heart and allow His resources to flow through our lives to the rest of God's family.

1. **Match the definitions on the right with the terms on the left.**

___ 1. Sharing	a. The joining of two lives for a common purpose
___ 2. Stewardship	b. Releasing everything in you to help others
___ 3. Partnership	c. Allowing God's resources to flow through your life to the rest of God's people

The essence of salvation can be found in the word *koinonia.* We fellowship with God intimately. We partner with God in His activity. We share in God's nature. We are given stewardship of that which belongs to God. We come to know God experientially. To describe an encounter with the living God defies human language; yet such an encounter is at the heart of what the New Testament writers tried to convey through the word *koinonia.*

2. **Read in your Bible 1 John 1:1-4 and answer the following questions.**

   a. Why did the disciples testify to the early church what they saw and heard in their relationship with Jesus?

   ____

   b. What is the result of being in fellowship with God and His people?

   ____

True *koinonia,* in its fullest expression, can be found in only one place—the local church. Nowhere else is God's love displayed and experienced more deeply than in the midst of His people as they gather. God delights to see His children gathering for worship, walking with one another, helping one another through life's journey, and serving Him with a unified heart. Jesus prayed "that they all may be one, as You, Father, are in Me, and I in You" (John 17:21). *Koinonia* is the answer to that prayer.

3. **Which of the following best describes your current experience of *koinonia?***

   ○ a. I experience *koinonia* with God and His people in many ways.
   ○ b. I occasionally experience *koinonia* but not very often.
   ○ c. I'm not sure I experience any *koinonia* in my life.

Conclude today's lesson by talking with God about your personal experience of *koinonia*. Ask the Lord to make you someone through whom true *koinonia* is expressed toward all of your church family.

Stewardship

1 Corinthians 15:10

"By God's grace I am what I am, and His grace toward me was not ineffective. However, I worked more than any of them, yet not I, but God's grace that was with me."

#1 answers: 1-b, 2-c, 3-a

#2 answers:
a–So that they would have fellowship together
b–Our joy is full/complete.

Day 4 • Dangers to Avoid

Read and meditate on "God's Word for Today" and "Today's Spiritual Reality" in the margin. Begin today's study with prayer.

Koinonia, like love, cannot be taken for granted. It requires determined involvement in one another's lives. Take a look at some dangers that damage the *koinonia* of a church.

Busyness. Sometimes we are so busy doing things for God that we don't have time with God. Remember, our fellowship with God is the key to having fellowship with one another. If the primary relationship fails, everything fails. And a grave danger is to be so busy with activities in the church that we neglect our relationships with God and His people.

Distractions. There are many good activities in a church, but we must keep the main thing the main thing—growing in our love relationship with God and building up the body. Many people find themselves in activities that either take them away from the church or keep them busy on the fringe. Before they know it, they wander away and are no longer involved.

1 **In the margin, list common distractions that frequently keep Christians away from regular involvement in their local church. We've given you some examples. Circle any distractions you need to deal with in your own life.**

Carelessness. People have a natural tendency to take relationships for granted. Only when something is taken away do we realize what we had. Or perhaps when a person is no longer around, we wish we had spent more time together. Christians need to value people and relationships. Don't neglect what God has given you. Nurture it and help it grow.

Disobedience. Sometimes believers choose to disobey God or to overlook sin that has crept into the fellowship. This usually begins as something small that doesn't seem to be too important. But sin, no matter how big or small, always eats away at fellowship. When we sin and willingly disobey God, we are kept from experiencing His blessing. Individual members cannot sin in isolation. Their sin will impact others within the fellowship.

God's Word for Today

"Do nothing out of rivalry or conceit, but in humility consider others as more important than yourselves." Philippians 2:3

Today's Spiritual Reality

Protect the fellowship at all costs.

Common Distractions

- Hobbies
- Children's sports
- Entertainment
- ________________

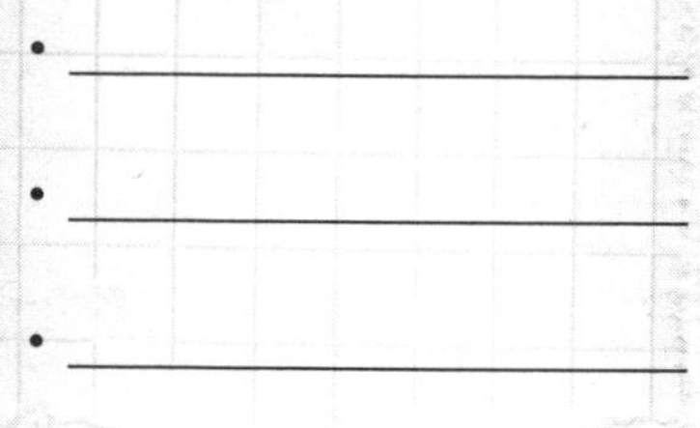

- ________________
- ________________
- ________________
- ________________
- ________________

Unforgiveness. Nothing can kill *koinonia* faster than bitterness harbored toward another person. Unforgiveness grows like a self-inflicted cancer of the heart. It separates people from one another and from God. God has forgiven you; you must freely forgive others. Don't be concerned with who was right or wrong; it's not worth it. Forgive, just as God has forgiven you.

Self-centeredness. This is the opposite of *koinonia.* To put yourself above others or to always want things your way will damage fellowship. Symptoms of being self-centered include easily getting offended, quickly getting angry, and being negative toward and critical of others. Often a self-centered person is jealous of others who are honored. The essence of sin is a self-centered nature that puts self before others, even before God.

Philippians 2:2-4
"Fulfill my joy by thinking the same way, having the same love, sharing the same feelings, focusing on one goal. Do nothing out of rivalry or conceit, but in humility consider others as more important than yourselves. Everyone should look out not only for his own interests, but also for the interests of others."

2. **Read Philippians 2:2-4. In the margin write a one-sentence summary of the way believers should focus on others.**

Summary

3. **Consider the dangers listed today's study. Which one(s) do you struggle with most and how?**

Maintaining close fellowship with the Lord is the key to keeping fellowship with one another. His presence in your life impacts all other relationships. Addressing the lukewarm, indifferent, self-centered church in Laodicea, Jesus essentially said, "If you want to experience fellowship with me in your church, just open the door" (see Revelation 3:20). It is not difficult; just let Him in! If you are thinking, *I need to go find a church that is enjoying true* koinonia, first ask yourself whether you need to stay where you are and be the one to open the door for your church. You can experience sweet fellowship with Christ even in a sick church. God may have put you in your church so that He could work through you to express His love to the rest of the church. If one person recognizes that it is Jesus who is knocking and that person opens the door, He will come in. Once He is in, He can begin to affect every part of the church through that person's life. Don't leave the church; the church needs you. Through one life *koinonia* love can begin to touch everybody in the church. Are you willing to be that person?

Revelation 3:20
"Listen! I stand at the door and knock. If anyone hears My voice and opens the door, I will come in to him and have dinner with him, and he with Me."

Conclude today's lesson by talking with God about the dangers you observe in your own life and church. Open the door and invite Jesus to come in and dine with you and influence your church's health.

Day 5 • The Testimony of Fellowship

Read and meditate on "God's Word for Today" and "Today's Spiritual Reality" in the margin. Begin today's study with prayer.

There is no more powerful force in the world than a church that enjoys *koinonia* with God and one another. *Koinonia* brings glory to God. It allows His blessings to flow among His people. And it is a powerful witness that demonstrates God's love to a watching world. Living God's great salvation among His people is God's strategy to touch a lost world and extend the Kingdom. When a church experiences *koinonia* as God intended, there is no limit to what He can do through them.

God's Word for Today
"Live your life in a manner worthy of the gospel of Christ." Philippians 1:27

Today's Spiritual Reality
Your relationship with the church accurately reflects your relationship with God.

1. **Which statements describe what happens through a church that enjoys *koinonia* with God and one another? Check all that apply.**
   ○ a. Makes a church act "holier than thou" ○ b. Glorifies God
   ○ c. Demonstrates God's love to the world ○ d. Blesses God's people

Can you see why the Bible makes so many strong statements about fellowship in the church? Paul said, "Live your life in a manner worthy of the gospel of Christ" (Philippians 1:27). The gospel is the story of the Lord's sacrifice, forfeiting what was rightfully His so that we could be saved. It is the story of His humility, setting aside His glory for us. It is the story of His forgiveness, paying for our sin so that we could stand before God in holiness. The gospel is the story of God's love in action—*koinonia.*

The gospel is the story of God's love in action—*koinonia.*

The reason Christ wants us to pay careful attention to our relationships with other people is that they are a barometer measuring our standing in our relationship with Him. Are there broken relationships in your life? Are there people you avoid because you have offended them? In Matthew 5:23-24 Jesus explained that our offerings and worship are not acceptable to Him unless we have been reconciled.

Matthew 5:23-24
"If you are offering your gift on the altar, and there you remember that your brother has something against you, leave your gift there in front of the altar. First go and be reconciled with your brother, and then come and offer your gift."

Did Jesus really mean what He said? Absolutely. Religious activity does not take precedence over *koinonia.* To continue your regular church activities when brokenness abounds is to live a lie. We must take Jesus seriously if we want to know *koinonia* as He intended. Trust Him on this; the blessings to be received from God are well worth the effort to make things right with others.

#1 answers: b, c, d

Jesus said in Matthew 9:13, "I desire mercy and not sacrifice." Sacrifice, religious duty, and acts of service are given to our deserving God. Mercy, kindness, and patience are given to people who are undeserving. God finds greater pleasure in watching us love one another as imperfect people than He does in receiving our love expressed through sacrifice. Mercy is an internal response that shows the true condition of the heart. He desires that.

1 John 4:7-11
"Let us love one another, because love is from God, and everyone who loves has been born of God and knows God. The one who does not love does not know God, because God is love. God's love was revealed among us in this way: God sent His One and Only Son into the world so that we might live through Him. Love consists in this: not that we loved God, but that He loved us and sent His Son to be the propitiation for our sins. Dear friends, if God loved us in this way, we also must love one another."

2 **Read 1 John 4:7-11 in the margin and circle the words *love, loves,* and *loved* every time you see them. Then answer the following questions.**

a. How did God love you? ______________________________

____

b. Why are we to love one another? ______________________________

____

c. What does it mean if we do not love one another? ______________

____

#2 answers:
a–Sent His Son to pay for my sin
b–Because God is love and we are born of Him; also because He loved us
c–We do not know God.

Jesus gave a wonderful promise in Luke 6:38: "Give, and it will be given to you; a good measure—pressed down, shaken together, and running over—will be poured into your lap. For with the measure you use, it will be measured back to you." Do you want forgiveness from God? Forgive others. Do you want mercy from God? Give mercy to others. Do you want grace from God? Extend grace to others. Do you want blessings from God? Generously bless others. Do you want to experience God's love in all its fullness? Lavish love on those around you.

Don't just look for a church with good fellowship. Be in fellowship with God and find ways to express your experience with God to those in your church. Then watch Him produce fellowship deeper than you have ever known.

Ask the Lord to make you a channel of His love in your church.

Review this week's lessons and underline the statement or Scripture God seemed to emphasize to you the most. Ask the Lord to show you how He wants you to respond to Him and to His people in light of what He has said to you this week. Write in the margin a prayer of response to the Lord.

Responding to the Lord

Session 4 • *Koinonia:* God's Love Expressed

Use some or all of the following suggestions to guide your small-group experience this week.

Opening Prayer

Building Relationships

Share *one* of the following with your group.

1. Describe a time when you experienced a special closeness to God.
2. Describe a time when you experienced a special closeness to your church family or to another member of the body of Christ.

Responding to Learning Activities

Share your responses to some or all of the following learning activities.

- Page 55, activity 2
- Page 59, activity 3. Why?

Reviewing Week 4

1. In pairs or triads take turns reciting your Scripture-memory verse, 1 John 1:7
2. Review this week's daily spiritual realities, reproduced below. Which one do you think identifies a reality you and your church most need to develop more fully so that you will experience God's best as a fellowship of believers? Why?
   - Day 1: We can have intimate fellowship with God.
   - Day 2: God expects us to have sincere fellowship with one another.
   - Day 3: As we receive from God, we give to the people of God.
   - Day 4: Protect the fellowship at all costs.
   - Day 5: Your relationship with the church accurately reflects your relationship with God.
3. How would you describe the biblical term *koinonia* (day 1 and p. 54, activity 1)?
4. What does *koinonia* look like in a church among the members?
5. List and describe some ways Scriptures instructs us to relate to one another (pp. 100–101). Which two or three would you most like to see practiced more in your church family? Why?

6. What is the best way to help God's people reconcile with one another (day 2 and p. 56, activity 2)?
7. How would you describe the place and importance of forgiveness in maintaining *koinonia* (day 2)?
8. How would you define partnership, sharing, and stewardship with regard to their role in experiencing *koinonia* (day 3)?
9. What are six dangers to avoid that would damage *koinonia* in your personal and church experience? What do you believe are the greatest dangers to fellowship in your church? In your life?
10. What happens through the testimony of a church that is experiencing *koinonia* with God and one another (day 5)?

Building Up the Body

1. During your review at the end of day 5, what statement or Scripture did you identify that you think God emphasized most this week?
2. Which truth that you have studied this week do you think would do the most to build up the body of Christ if you and other members of your church faithfully applied it?
3. How do you want to respond to what you have learned this week? How has the Lord prompted you this week to love His people and build up His body?

Praying Together

Volunteers, pray sentence or brief prayers for one another and for your church, based on what you've shared today.

- Pray specifically to experience intimacy with God.
- Pray for reconciliation of all broken relationships in the body and for unity.
- Pray that you will remove distractions and change other behaviors that hinder the experience of *koinonia*.

Preview Week 5

Turn to page 67 and preview the study for the coming week.

Week 5

Loving One Another

"I give you a new commandment: love one another. Just as I have loved you, you must also love one another."

John 13:34

Loving One Another

OVERVIEW OF WEEK 5

Day 1: By Nature
Day 2: Commanded to Love
Day 3: Love like Jesus, Part 1
Day 4: Love like Jesus, Part 2
Day 5: Committed to Love

VERSE TO MEMORIZE

"I give you a new commandment: love one another. Just as I have loved you, you must also love one another" (John 13:34).

DISCIPLESHIP HELP FOR WEEK 5

"The Love Test" (pp. 102–3)

POSSIBLE RESPONSES TO WEEK 5

As I learn how to obey Jesus' command to love one another, I will respond by doing things like the following.

- I will increasingly surrender to the Holy Spirit's work in my life so that His fruit of love will be revealed in my actions and attitudes.
- I will seek the welfare of others without regard to their worthiness.
- I choose to obey Christ's command to love, and I will let Him set the standards and reveal the opportunities and the recipients.
- I will watch for and respond to God's invitations for me to lay down things I claim as my own in order to demonstrate love toward brothers and sisters in Christ.
- I will choose to forgive and seek reconciliation to avoid any division that would violate the love in my church family.
- I will find at least two practical ways to show Christ's love to someone in my church family this week.
- I will fully commit myself to loving involvement in my church with no anticipation of abandoning my church if tough times come.
- I will not wait for others to love me. I will proactively look for people in my church to love this week.

Day 1 • By Nature

Read and meditate on "God's Word for Today" and "Today's Spiritual Reality" in the margin. Begin today's study with prayer.

Our church has many young, growing families; so celebrating the birth of a child is a regular occurrence! It is fascinating to watch as these children grow to be like their parents. In many cases you could identify the child's parents simply by observing the child. The reason is simple: each child is by nature and by nurture like his or her parents.

Our Heavenly Father has the same kind of expectation for those who have been spiritually born again. Because we are His children, our lives should exhibit His characteristics. In Galatians 5:22-23 Paul identified the fruit of the Spirit, the characteristics of God that should be expressed in and through our lives because His Spirit dwells in us. For example, patience is one fruit of the Spirit. We who are learning to follow Christ readily recognize the great patience that the Lord shows His children. As we choose to walk by His Spirit, His patience will increasingly characterize our lives and behaviors.

1. **Read Galatians 5:22-23 in the margin and circle the fruit of the Spirit.**

2. **If a Christlike believer observed your life long enough, what do you think he would conclude about your relationship with God? Check one or write your own.**
   - ○ a. "I clearly see fruit in your life that leads me to believe the Spirit of Christ lives in you."
   - ○ b. "The fruit of the Spirit is not strong or clear in your life. I assume you are either young in your faith, immature, or tainted by sin."
   - ○ c. "I don't see any evidence of the Spirit's fruit. Have you really been born again by the Spirit?"
   - ○ d. Other: ____

   ____

The one characteristic of God that defines all the others is love. It is not just that God is very loving; God *is* love*. Our Heavenly Father's very nature is love—perfect love. Therefore, because we are His children, our lives should be characterized by His love. In fact, if we do not love, the authenticity

God's Word for Today

"We know that we have passed from death to life because we love our brothers. The one who does not love remains in death." 1 John 3:14

Today's Spiritual Reality

God's nature should characterize the lives of His children.

Galatians 5:22-23

"The fruit of the Spirit is love, joy, peace, patience, kindness, goodness, faith, gentleness, self-control. Against such things there is no law."

* ***love:*** the essential nature of God, a choice that seeks the welfare of others without regard to their worthiness

of our relationship with God can be questioned (see 1 John 4:8). Because God is love, the lives of His children should be characterized by love.

1 John 4:8
"The one who does not love does not know God, because God is love."

3 **Read again the definition of *love* on the previous page. Write a definition of *love* in your own words.**

____

____

Love is an action and not just a feeling. When we love, we show it. God loved us, so He sent His Son to pay our sin debt on the cross. We had a need, and He met our need. He didn't just feel lovingly toward us; He did something that showed us His love.

Love is an action and not just a feeling.

On the night before Jesus went to the cross, He issued a new command that His disciples love one another (see John 13:34). The fact that He restated this command twice to His disciples indicates that loving one another is absolutely crucial to the heart of God. Jesus defined the way we are to love one another: "just as I have loved you." On our own it is impossible to love as Jesus loves. Because we are born of God, however, He intends for us to display His nature of love.

John 13:34
"I give you a new commandment: love one another. Just as I have loved you, you must also love one another."

The first place this love should be expressed is among other believers—the family of God. A family without love is dysfunctional and full of pain. This is true not only humanly but also spiritually. When we were born spiritually, God placed us in a spiritual family. Within this family God's love should be expressed through us and toward one another.

Sometimes it seems that our church family gets the least amount of our love. Sadly, our churches are often characterized by division and conflict instead of Jesus' love. This situation should cause us to tremble! Love toward one another ought to be the natural outflow of a life that has been born of God.

Love toward one another ought to be the natural outflow of a life that has been born of God.

Conclude today's lesson by talking with God about the quality of His love you see in your life. If it doesn't look much like His love, ask Him to reveal the reason and help you get yourself out of the way so that His love can shine through your life. Ask Him to teach you this week how to love others the way He has loved you.

Day 2 • Commanded to Love

God's Word for Today
"This is His command: that we believe in the name of His Son Jesus Christ, and love one another as He commanded us." 1 John 3:23

Today's Spiritual Reality
To love one another is a command from our Lord that must be obeyed.

Read and meditate on "God's Word for Today" and "Today's Spiritual Reality" in the margin. Begin today's study with prayer.

There is a big difference between a suggestion and a command. A suggestion is advice that may help someone through a situation. The person is not obligated to take the advice; it is simply offered in hopes of helping. A command, on the other hand, is given to a subordinate with the expectation that the person will obey. If the subordinate does not obey, discipline follows.

1. **Write a *C* beside the descriptions below that relate to commands. Write an *S* beside those related to suggestions.**
   ___ a. Advice that may help you if followed
   ___ b. Expection given by someone in authority that calls for obedience
   ___ c. Mandatory
   ___ d. Optional

#1 answers: C=b,c; S=a,d

Many Christians view God's commands as suggestions to live a better life. But God did not issue suggestions to His people; He gave us commands. The way we respond to these commands reveals the nature of our relationship with Him. Jesus once asked, "Why do you call Me 'Lord, Lord,' and don't do the things I say?" (Luke 6:46). In other words, we can say Jesus is the Lord of our lives, but true lordship is revealed in the way we respond to His commands. We honor Him as Lord when we obey His commands.

2. **Which describes the way you have approached loving God's people?**
   ○ a. I understand that it is a command, and I seek to obey Him.
   ○ b. I view it more as a suggestion to follow if it is convenient.

1 Peter 3:15
"Set apart the Messiah as Lord in your hearts."

Philippians 2:13
"It is God who is working in you, enabling you both to will and to act for His good purpose."

John 15:17
"This is what I command you: love one another."

Read 1 Peter 3:15 and Philippians 2:13 in the margin. Take time now and express to Christ your desire to obey Him as the Lord of your life from this day forward. Ask Him for strength to obey.

Jesus made absolutely certain His disciples understood that to love one another was not a suggestion but a commandment (see John 15:17). Every time He told them to love one another, He clarified that this was a commandment. As the apostle John reflected on this in his letters, he clearly stated that to love one another was not optional for a child of God (see 1 John 2:3). As a command given directly by Christ, it should be obeyed.

Those who have truly been born again and have made Christ the Lord of their lives will seek to obey His commands. In 2 Corinthians 5:14-15 the apostle Paul said the love of Christ compelled or gripped his life. As he reflected on what Jesus had done for him, Paul concluded that there was only one response: "That those who live should no longer live for themselves, but for the One who died for them and was raised." As we reflect on what Jesus has done for us, our natural response should be to love and obey Him as Lord, choosing to live for Him and not for ourselves.

Yesterday we learned that our capacity to love one another comes from being born of God. As His children, we have His Spirit and, thus, His nature in us. This does not mean we will obey His command to love one another without effort. Even though we have the capacity to love, we must still choose to love. Obedience to Christ and His commands is a choice we must make as a love response to our Lord.

This choice will reveal whether we are living in a relationship with Christ. Obedience is the indicator that we know Him and that we love Him (see John 14:21). This indicator is displayed no more plainly than in the way we relate to our brothers and sisters in Christ.

As children of God, we continually seek to find ways to show God's love to our brothers and sisters in Christ. To love the people of God is not a casual thing but a command to be obeyed in response to our Lord. Those who obey this command to love the people of God are filled with joy because they experience their Lord in a deep, profound way.

(3) **List at least two practical ways you can obey your Lord and show His love to people in your church family. Read the list in the margin if you need to jump-start your thinking. Think about needs you can meet.**

____

____

Conclude today's lesson by talking with God about your obedience to love as He loved. Ask Him to guide and enable your loving others.

1 John 2:3
"This is how we are sure that we have come to know Him: by keeping His commands."

Those who have truly been born again and have made Christ the Lord of their lives will seek to obey His commands.

John 14:21
"The one who has My commands and keeps them is the one who loves Me."

Suggestions for Loving One Another

- Encouraging the discouraged
- Visiting the sick
- Spending time with the lonely
- Praying for the confused
- Feeding the hungry
- Providing finances or material help for the needy
- Comforting the grieving
- Giving a job to the unemployed
- Seeking justice for the oppressed
- Assisting with house and yard work during an illness

God's Word for Today

"I give you a new command-ment: love one another. Just as I have loved you, you must also love one another."
John 13:34

Today's Spiritual Reality

To love like Jesus requires sacrifice and steadfastness.

Christ's Love for Me

Common Needs

Day 3 • Love like Jesus, Part 1

Read and meditate on "God's Word for Today" and "Today's Spiritual Reality" in the margin. Begin today's study with prayer.

If Jesus' command were simply to love one another as best we can, anyone could do it. But He is very specific about how we are to love one another. His requirement is that we love just as He has loved us. This kind of love goes far beyond our own ability. To love as He loves requires loving with His love. It requires that we live in a relationship with Christ and that He pour His love into our lives.

How has Jesus loved us? We will never be able to fully answer that question. In fact, Paul said in Ephesians 3:19 that the love of Christ "surpasses knowledge." But we can identify many aspects of Jesus' love in order to better obey Him and love one another. Today we will focus on two.

Jesus' love for us is sacrificial. When we think of Christ's love, we think of the cross and His sacrifice for us. Paul wrote in Romans 5:8, "God proves His own love for us in that while we were still sinners Christ died for us!" God's love was most clearly displayed on the cross.

1. **Draw a simple picture in the margin under "Christ's Love for Me" of Jesus on the cross with a broken body and shed blood. As you draw your picture, reflect on the pain and suffering He endured for you.**

God gives us many opportunities to show His love to one another through sacrifice. Several times in Acts we see that those in the first church eagerly sacrificed to meet the need of others (see Acts 4:32-37). They seem to have relished the opportunity to sacrifice for one another. They sold property to share the resources with others who had need. When they saw a brother in need, they made an effort to meet that need.

2. **List in the margin some common needs of individuals and families you have observed in the body of Christ.**

Christ wants us to have the same attitude as the first church. He does not want us to avoid sacrifice for one another but to embrace it. Through sacrifice we can show Christ's love toward a brother or a sister in need. If we love like Jesus, we will place others above ourselves and look for opportunities to meet their needs. Will you love God's people no matter the personal cost? We should even willingly lay down our lives for our brothers and sisters in Christ (see 1 John 3:16). Though that doesn't seem likely to be required of us in North America, many around the world are laying down their physical lives for Christ's sake. However, you may have an opportunity to lay down other things because of your love for your church family.

1 John 3:16
"This is how we have come to know love: He laid down His life for us. We should also lay down our lives for our brothers."

3. **Does God want you to lay down or give away any of the following? Check any that He speaks to you about or write your own in the margin.[1]**

- ○ A material possession
- ○ Your preferences, opinions
- ○ A preferred schedule
- ○ Time to serve others
- ○ Resistance to change
- ○ Opposition to a project
- ○ Withholding of support
- ○ Money
- ○ Your dreams, goals, desires
- ○ An activity or program
- ○ A position of leadership
- ○ Your comfort or security
- ○ Your rights
- ○ Your reputation

Jesus' love for us is steadfast. Most Christians cling to the Lord's promise that He will always be with us (see Matthew 28:20). His constant presence through His Spirit is one of the deepest expressions of His love. In His abiding presence we find joy, peace, and rest. We don't have to worry that one day He will stop loving us and leave. Unfortunately, we seldom think twice about severing a relationship because we are not getting out of it all we want. God does not intend for the church to act like this. His purpose for His people is that we commit ourselves to Him *and* to one another.

Matthew 28:20
"I am with you always, to the end of the age."

Recently, the Lord called our church to walk with several churches through a crisis. It is heartbreaking to hear them speak of the pain they experience as members leave because of difficulties. One man said, "The pain is so deep because those who left were not simply friends or acquaintances; they were family." To love as Jesus loves requires that we commit to our church family with all our heart, promising to be there in good times and bad.

To love as Jesus loves requires that we commit to our church family with all our heart, promising to be there in good times and bad.

Conclude today's lesson by talking with God about sacrifice and steadfastness. Thank the Lord for His sacrifice for you. Ask Him to show you how you can sacrificially love those in your church body. Ask Him to build steadfast love in your church family as well.

1. Adapted from Claude King, *Come to the Lord's Table* (Nashville: LifeWay Press, 2006), 89. Used by permission.

Day 4 • Love like Jesus, Part 2

God's Word for Today
"This is My command: love one another as I have loved you."
John 15:12

Today's Spiritual Reality
To love like Jesus means that we forgive, show His love unconditionally, and initiate loving others.

Read and meditate on "God's Word for Today" and "Today's Spiritual Reality" in the margin. Begin today's study with prayer.

Yesterday we learned that Jesus doesn't simply command us to love one another; He commands us to love one another just as He has loved us. But we cannot love like Him in our own power or ability. The only way to love like Jesus is to live in an abiding relationship with Him. There He equips us to love one another with His love. We also looked at sacrifice and steadfastness as two crucial characteristics of Jesus' love that we should express toward one another. Today we will focus on three more characteristics of Jesus' love.

Jesus' love is expressed through forgiveness. Christ has forgiven us far beyond anything we can ever comprehend. To deal with our sin cost Him dearly; yet He forgives freely and completely. Jesus is eager to deal with our sin and to deal with it completely, because He understands better than anyone else the cost of unforgiven sin. In last week's study on *koinonia,* we learned that God expects us to forgive others if we are to be forgiven by Him (see Matthew 6:14-15, p. 57). Our forgiveness of others affects our fellowship with God. Today we want to focus on our forgiveness of others as a demonstration of Jesus' love.

1 John 1:9
"If we will confess our sins, He is faithful and righteous to forgive us our sins and to cleanse us from all unrighteousness."

Read 1 John 1:9 in the margin. Thank the Lord for doing all that was needed to forgive you of your sin.

God intends for His people to be characterized by His forgiveness. Church members should readily forgive one another as they have been forgiven (see Ephesians 4:32). Yet often our churches are full of broken relationships because members refuse to forgive. A church will never be able to fully function as the body of Christ as long as members are unwilling to forgive. If we love one another like Jesus, we are eager to forgive.

Ephesians 4:32
"Be kind and compassionate to one another, forgiving one another, just as God also forgave you in Christ."

1 **Mark the following statements *T* for *true* or *F* for *false*.**

__ 1. We need Jesus' forgiveness, but we do not need to forgive one another.

__ 2. A church will struggle to function if members refuse to forgive.

__ 3. Those who love like Jesus eagerly show forgiveness to one another.

#1 answers: 1-F; 2-T; 3-T

Jesus' love is given without merit. Aren't you glad Jesus did not wait for you to deserve His love before He loved you? God's love is not earned; it is humbly accepted as a free gift of His grace. Each of us deserves death and condemnation because we have all sinned (see Romans 3:23). Yet because of God's great love, He sought to save us and give us life in His Son.

Romans 3:23
"All have sinned and fall short of the glory of God."

The truth of God's love and grace should influence the way we love one another. As God's children, we must show unmerited love toward one another. Jesus rushed into our lives with His love when we least deserved it. To love like Jesus requires that we show His love toward all the people of God, even those who seem the most undeserving.

Jesus initiates His love toward us. God initiated the expression of His love toward us when He sent His Son (see Romans 5:6). Instead of waiting for us to come to Him, He was proactive. Even in the lives of His children, His Spirit constantly works to apply His love and to draw us closer to Him. He continually initiates His love toward us!

Romans 5:6
"While we were still helpless, at the appointed moment, Christ died for the ungodly."

Many of us sit back in church and wait to be loved by others. We rationalize that when we are loved, we will love back. To love like Jesus requires us to be proactive in showing His love. Instead of sitting back and waiting on others, we must initiate relationships with the people of God.

(2) **Which best describes your attitude? Check one or write your own.**
○ a. I am proactive in showing Christ's love to others in my church.
○ b. I show love only toward those who really seem to deserve it.
○ c. I show love only to those who have already shown love to me.
○ d. Other: ______________________________

(3) **Ask the Lord to show you specific people in your church whom He wants you to love this week. List them in the margin and note what you need to do to demonstrate Jesus' love to them.**

(4) **Turn to pages 102–3 in "Discipleship Helps" and complete "The Love Test" to measure your love against Paul's description in 1 Corinthians 13.**

Conclude today's lesson by talking with God about the way you show His love to others. Ask Him to fill you with His love so that it will naturally overflow into the lives of others, especially in your church.

Day 5 • Committed to Love

God's Word for Today

"All the believers were together and had everything in common. So they sold their possessions and property and distributed the proceeds to all, as anyone had a need."
Acts 2:44-45

Today's Spiritual Reality

To love one another, we must be absolutely committed to our church family.

Read and meditate on "God's Word for Today" and "Today's Spiritual Reality" in the margin. Begin today's study with prayer.

True commitment is a rare gem in our society. People seem to avoid commitment whenever possible. For example, more and more couples are choosing to live together instead of getting married. They've decided to leave the back door open, actually anticipating that their commitment will some day come to an end. The thought of a lifelong commitment is beyond their imagination. The result is often pain, heartbreak, and shallow relationships, because God designed us for committed relationships. Commitment is at the heart of every genuine love relationship.

Unfortunately, a lack of commitment has found its way into Christianity, deeply affecting churches. Many believers look for a church that will meet their expectations and needs. Then they settle in and enjoy the ride. When the situation or their needs change, however, they simply move on to another church. Little or no thought is given to making a commitment to the people of God in the local church. They hesitate to build deep friendships or assume responsibilities that might tie them down. Then they use their own human reasoning to make a move rather than seek God's directions for their involvement in His church.

1. **If you were honest with yourself, which of the following would best describe your commitment to your church family? Check one or write your own.**

○ a. I'm keeping my options open. I'll stick around as long as my needs are being met. I'm not too close to others, because I don't want to get hurt if I make a move.

○ b. I'm all in. I'm loving my church family and believing I'll never leave. I'm putting down roots in my relationships and accepting opportunities to serve. I'm here for the long haul, even if tough times come.

○ c. Other: ______________________________

____

____

For centuries believers have pointed to the first church as the model for all churches. The first church experienced God moving powerfully in and through them. They witnessed thousands of people respond to the gospel in faith as the Spirit of God moved among them. What was it about the first church that allowed the Lord to use it so powerfully?

2 **As you read the following paragraph, underline two facts about the commitments of the early church in Jerusalem.**

As we study the first church in Jerusalem, two facts rise to the surface. First, the people were totally committed to the Lord and His plan. Second, they were totally committed to one another. We tend to separate these two commitments. In reality, one is expressed by the other. Our commitment in love to the Lord will be expressed by our commitment to love one another, because these members are the body of Christ today. We show love for Christ when we love His body. The first church clearly understood this necessity.

For our churches to be what God intends, we must be committed to the Lord and to one another. Most of us want to be committed to the Lord but hesitate to commit to His people. These two commitments are inseparable.

We may not always agree on everything, but we are family; we stick together. As the Father has loved us, so we love one another.

As Christians, we cannot stand outside the church and watch from a distance. Love compels us to be involved. We cannot mock the church, laugh at it, or call it a hypocrite. That runs against every fiber of our faith. Those who have been born again love the church and give their lives for it. We may not always agree on everything, but we are family; we stick together. As the Father has loved us, so we love one another.

Responding to the Lord

Have you been committed to the Lord but not to His people? Spend time with Him in prayer asking Him to show you whether you are as committed to His people as He desires.

Review this week's lessons and underline the statement or Scripture God seemed to emphasize to you the most. Ask the Lord to show you how He wants you to respond to Him and to His people in light of what He has said to you this week. Write in the margin a prayer of response to the Lord.

Session 5 • Loving One Another

Use some or all of the following suggestions to guide your small-group experience this week.

Opening Prayer

Building Relationships

Share *one* of the following with your group.

1. Describe a time when you experienced love through the body of Christ because others met your need.
2. Describe a time when you experienced the beauty and joy of reconciliation by forgiving someone or receiving their forgiveness.
3. Describe a time when you were offended and have not been able to forgive. Ask the group to pray for you to be able to forgive with Christ's help. Group: Pray aloud for this request before moving to the next person.

Responding to Learning Activities

Share your responses to some or all of the following learning activities.

- Page 68, activity 2
- Page 73, activity 3
- Page 75, activities 2 and 3
- Page 76, activity 1. Why?

Reviewing Week 5

1. In pairs or triads take turns reciting your Scripture-memory verse, John 13:34.
2. Review this week's daily spiritual realities, reproduced below. Which one do you think identifies a reality you and your church most need to develop more fully so that you will experience God's best as a fellowship of believers? Why?
   - Day 1: God's nature should characterize the lives of His children.
   - Day 2: To love one another is a command from our Lord that must be obeyed.
   - Day 3: To love like Jesus requires sacrifice and steadfastness.
   - Day 4: To love like Jesus means that we forgive, show His love unconditionally, and initiate loving others.
   - Day 5: To love one another, we must be absolutely committed to our church family.

3. How would you define *love* in your own words (p. 69, activity 3)?
4. What is the difference between a command and a suggestion? Which term describes Jesus' words in John 13:34? How should we respond to Him (day 2)?
5. List practical ways you can show Christ's love to people in your church family (p. 71, activity 3 and p. 103, activity 2).
6. Name five characteristics of Jesus' love for us. For each characteristic give an example of how we can love others in a Christlike manner (days 3–4).
7. What are some ways the early church showed its commitment to one another (p. 77, activity 2 and the Book of Acts)?

Building Up the Body

1. During your review at the end of day 5, what statement or Scripture did you identify that you think God emphasized most this week?
2. Which truth that you have studied this week do you think would do the most to build up the body of Christ if you and other members of your church faithfully applied it?
3. How do you want to respond to what you have learned this week? How has the Lord prompted you this week to love His people and build up His body?
4. Review the courses in the Growing Disciples Series on page 110 and identify possible next steps in your personal and church's growth in following Christ. Which course would be most helpful? Why?

Praying Together

Pray sentence or brief prayers for one another, based on what you've shared today. Pray for those with special needs. Pray that God will guide and strengthen members to demonstrate Christ's love. Pray that your lives and your church will begin to overflow with expressions of His love.

Preview Week 6

1. Turn to page 81 and preview the study for the coming week.
2. Leader: If your church has not already done so, identify one or more courses of study you will offer members as next steps in their growth in discipleship. To discover options, look at the resources described at *www.lifeway.com/discipleship*.

Week 6

Bearing One Another's Burdens

"Carry one another's
burdens; in this way you
will fulfill the law of Christ."
Galatians 6:2

Bearing One Another's Burdens

OVERVIEW OF WEEK 6

Day 1: Living in a Fallen World
Day 2: Physical Burdens
Day 3: Spiritual Burdens
Day 4: The Power of the Tongue
Day 5: Keeping the Unity of the Spirit

VERSE TO MEMORIZE

"Carry one another's burdens; in this way you will fulfill the law of Christ" (Galatians 6:2).

POSSIBLE RESPONSES TO WEEK 6

As I accept responsibility for bearing the physical and spiritual burdens of others in the body of Christ, I will respond by doing things like the following.

- I will seek to support those in my church because we need one another.
- I will ask the Lord to show me how I can tangibly help someone in my church family who is struggling with physical burdens.
- I will begin to reach out with Christ's love to those with spiritual burdens and help them find freedom in Christ.
- I will ask my pastor or a church leader how I can help him bear the burden of his God-given assignments.
- I will seek to use my words to encourage those in Christ's body. This week I will send at least two persons notes or e-mails of encouragement.
- I will seek to reconcile and unify those in the body who are at odds with one another.
- I will humbly reveal my own burdens and allow the members of the body of Christ to minister to me.

Day 1 • Living in a Fallen World

Read and meditate on "God's Word for Today" and "Today's Spiritual Reality" in the margin. Begin today's study with prayer.

Wouldn't it be great to live in a perfect world? There would be no problems to hold us back, and everyone would live in harmony. Unfortunately, our world is far from perfect. In fact, because of sin, this world has fallen from God's intended position. And that's just where God has placed us and our churches—in a fallen and corrupted world.

God's Word for Today
"Carry one another's burdens; in this way you will fulfill the law of Christ." Galatians 6:2

Today's Spiritual Reality
Because we live in a fallen world, we need one another.

1 **As you read the next two paragraphs, underline the reasons God has placed His church in a fallen world.**

The Spirit within us creates a longing for our spiritual home—that perfect place where Jesus rules over all things (see 2 Corinthians 5:8). We may long to be in heaven, but we are called by God to function as His body in this world. God placed His church in the middle of this fallen world for several reasons. One reason is that He wants the world's people to see Him and to know that He loves them. This happens as they see God's people loving one another, walking together in harmony, and bearing one another's burdens (see John 13:35).

2 Corinthians 5:8, NIV
"We are confident, I say, and would prefer to be away from the body and at home with the Lord."

John 13:35
"By this all people will know that you are My disciples, if you have love for one another."

Another reason God desires for us to function together as His church is the simple fact that we need one another. There's nothing worse than being alone and in desperate need of help. Our Heavenly Father intends for His children to help one another as we encounter difficulties in this world. This is why being part of His body is so important.

Some people in the church think we will encounter difficult times only when we are not following the Lord. It is true that God will discipline us when we are not following Him, but this isn't the only time difficulties arise. In fact, problems can develop in the healthiest churches. Often issues arise simply because life is difficult and people are imperfect. During these times we have the opportunity and privilege to help bear one another's burdens.

#1 answers: "He wants the world's people to see Him and to know that He loves them." "We need one another."

Acts 6:1 gives us a glimpse of a problem that arose in the early church: "In those days, as the number of the disciples was multiplying, there arose a complaint by the Hellenistic Jews against the Hebraic Jews that their widows were being overlooked in the daily distribution [of food]." Although God was moving powerfully and the early church was growing exponentially, "there arose a complaint." The problem didn't result from the church's sin. These believers were walking with the Lord. The reality of life is that believers will experience problems until Christ returns. Issues will arise in our churches, even those with godly leaders. The question is, Will we take advantage of these opportunities to help one another?

2. **Briefly describe in the margin a time in your church when a member faced a difficult situation and the church helped the person.**

Our Church's Experience

Some of us are guilty of constantly looking for the ideal church. There is only one problem: this church does not exist. Nevertheless, God has built and placed churches in a troubled world—churches filled with people He knew would face problems and difficulties. His intent is that we face the issues of this world together as we walk with Christ. This requires that we learn to bear one another's burdens.

Are you prepared to help bear the burdens of those God has placed in your church family? If so, that's great; but that's only one side of the relationship. Are you also willing to allow those in your church family to help you bear the burdens of your life? If we are to walk together as the body of Christ, we must be not only ready to help others but also willing for the Lord to work through others to help us.

3. **What burdens (if any) are you carrying right now? Briefly describe them in the margin.**

My Burdens

4. **Are you ready and willing to lay down your pride and allow the body of Christ to minister to you by helping you carry these burdens?**

Conclude today's lesson by talking with God about burdens you see in your church family and any you may be experiencing yourself. Ask the Lord to help you and your church be more sensitive to the opportunities He gives you to help one another. Give God permission to minister to your needs through your church family.

Day 2 • Physical Burdens

God's Word for Today
"Is anyone among you sick? He should call for the elders of the church, and they should pray over him after anointing him with olive oil in the name of the Lord." James 5:14

Today's Spiritual Reality
We need to help carry one another's physical burdens.

Read and meditate on "God's Word for Today" and "Today's Spiritual Reality" in the margin. Begin today's study with prayer.

Physical burdens are part of life in this fallen world. We all want to be as healthy as possible, but the sobering reality is that we are putting off the inevitable. Unless Christ returns, we will all succumb to the physical decay our bodies must endure in this world. Thankfully, as children of God, we look forward to the day when He will give us new bodies that will be free from physical decay. But for now we have physical burdens, and we need to help one another bear these burdens.

Some believe that any illness or physical defect must be the direct result of a person's failure with God. Illness and physical problems, however, are not always the result of sin. Frequently, they are just part of living in this fallen world. In John 9 Jesus approached a man born blind. His disciples assumed the man's blindness was the result of either his or his parents' sin. Jesus pointed out that it wasn't because of sin that the man was blind but rather "so that God's works might be displayed in him" (v. 3). We will have physical problems in this life. Believers must see these times as opportunities to walk with one another and to allow the Lord to be glorified through us.

(1) **Mark the following statements *T* for *true* or *F* for *false*.**

__ 1. All illness is the result of a person's failure with God.

__ 2. The physical problems we face in this world are opportunities for us to walk together and for the Lord to be glorified through us.

James 5 instructs us to pray for one another when illness arises. Often we have the attitude that prayer is the minimum we can do. Actually, it is the most powerful thing we can do if we are walking with the Lord. United prayer by the local church brings God-given power to the situation. If we are to truly bear one another's burdens, we must begin to take prayer as seriously as our Lord does. How quick are you to pray with and for someone in need?

United prayer by the local church brings God-given power to the situation.

I recently heard a pastor explain to a man that he couldn't commit to pray for him because he was busy and might forget. He didn't want the man to think he was praying for him when he was not. My first thought was that

#1 answers: 1-F, 2-T

the pastor could have taken time to pray with the man in less time than it took for him to explain why he could not! If we are to fulfill the law of Christ and bear one another's burdens, we must focus more of our attention toward the Lord in prayer on behalf of our brothers and sisters in Christ.

(2) **What is one way you can bear the physical burdens of others?**

____

James 2:15-16
"If a brother or sister is without clothes and lacks daily food, and one of you says to them, 'Go in peace, keep warm, and eat well,' but you don't give them what the body needs, what good is it?"

As important as prayer is to bearing the physical burdens of one another, we must not stop there. James challenged the early church not just to *recognize* the physical needs of their fellow brothers and sisters in Christ but also to seek to *meet* their needs (see James 2:15-16). Bearing one another's burdens means we come beside those in need and help them in ways the Lord shows us. This may mean cooking meals, doing lawn care, providing clothes, helping financially, or simply spending time with them. Our assignment from the Lord is to love one another with His love. This means we hold nothing back, counting it a privilege to help one another with what God has given us.

Bearing one another's burdens means we come beside those in need and help them in ways the Lord shows us.

(3) **The Lord has shaped you to build up His body through service. List two more ways you can help those in your church family with physical needs.**

____

____

My (Bo's) family has experienced the Lord's power and love as our church walked with us through physically difficult and frightening times. In these times we sensed the Lord's presence through His people. We can't imagine having gone through these times without our church family. They prayed for us, helped with our children, fed us, and took care of us in many different ways. The Lord accomplished His plan to meet our needs through the lives of His people.

Conclude today's lesson by talking with God about physical needs of which you are aware in your church family. Identify someone in your church who is struggling physically and pray for that person. Ask the Lord (and/or call the person to ask) what you can do to help meet his or her needs. (If you can't meet the needs alone, invite others to help you.)

Day 3 • Spiritual Burdens

Read and meditate on "God's Word for Today" and "Today's Spiritual Reality" in the margin. Begin today's study with prayer.

Bearing one another's spiritual burdens begins with praying for one another. As crucial as it is for us to help bear one another's physical burdens, helping those with spiritual burdens is even more important. Paul said our struggle is not simply against flesh and blood but against the spiritual forces controlled by the evil one. The body of Christ must be prepared to fight spiritual battles.

1. **Read Ephesians 6:12 in the margin and underline the ones with whom we do spiritual battle when we pray.**

Sometimes we can be lulled into a sense of peace and safety, forgetting that we are in a spiritual battle. The apostle Paul understood the reality of the battle he was involved in from the moment Jesus saved him. Subsequent years of following Christ taught him important truths about this battle.

Paul knew that the people of God were not to simply give one another moral support but were to stand together and fight spiritually. Listen to his instructions in Ephesians 6:18: "With every prayer and request, pray at all times in the Spirit, and stay alert in this, with all perseverance and intercession for all the saints." Paul knew the importance of praying for one another. When we seek the Lord on one another's behalf, He provides all we need for spiritual battle.

I (Bo) am moved when people let me know the Lord has led them to pray for me. Often it is in the midst of a spiritual issue or battle I have been facing, which they knew nothing about. In these times I need the spiritual support of God's people.

Paul was not giving the church in Ephesus instructions he was not following. Read Ephesians 6:19-20 in the margin. Paul knew he needed God's people to help him carry the spiritual burden that came with his call. The Lord had given him the huge assignment of carrying the gospel to the Gentiles. He could not do this in his own power; he needed the Lord to work through him, so he regularly asked God's people to pray for him.

God's Word for Today

"With every prayer and request, pray at all times in the Spirit, and stay alert in this, with all perseverance and intercession for all the saints."
Ephesians 6:18

Today's Spiritual Reality

We need to help carry one another's spiritual burdens.

Ephesians 6:12
"Our battle is not against flesh and blood, but against the rulers, against the authorities, against the world powers of this darkness, against the spiritual forces of evil in the heavens."

Ephesians 6:19-20
"Pray also for me, that the message may be given to me when I open my mouth to make known with boldness the mystery of the gospel. For this I am an ambassador in chains. Pray that I might be bold enough in Him to speak as I should."

Take a few minutes and pray the requests of Ephesians 6:19-20 for your pastor and others who preach, teach, and witness for Christ.

Paul's specific request was for people to pray that he would speak the truth of the gospel with boldness. This may seem like a strange request; we know Paul spoke the gospel with great boldness. But his boldness did not come from his personality; it came from God in answer to the prayers of the church. The body of Christ helped Paul bear this spiritual burden. In the same way, God intends for us to help one another carry the spiritual burdens that come with His assignments.

Suppose your small group asked you, "How may we pray for your spiritual burdens?" What would you request? Write it in the margin.

Jesus intends for His body, your church, to function the way He functions. During His earthly ministry the Pharisees struggled with the fact that He associated with sinners. Jesus' reply in Matthew 9:11-12 was that He came to help those who had deep spiritual burdens. Our church should be a place where those with spiritual burdens can come and find help and freedom.

Matthew 9:11-12
"When the Pharisees saw this, they asked His disciples, 'Why does your Teacher eat with tax collectors and sinners?' But when [Jesus] heard this, He said, 'Those who are well don't need a doctor, but the sick do.'"

③ **Which best describes your church?**

○ a. Trying to help those with spiritual burdens find freedom in Christ
○ b. Hesitant to support those with spiritual burdens
○ c. Desire to carry spiritual burdens but not sure how to do it
○ d. Other: ______________________________

I recently met a man named Joe who was once a drug addict. The Lord saved Joe and placed him in a church that cared for him and helped bear his burdens. As a result, God has set him free, redeemed his life, and now uses him powerfully to carry the spiritual burdens of others. This is what Jesus intends to happen when people come to our churches.

Our church should be a place where those with spiritual burdens can come and find help and freedom.

Conclude today's lesson by talking with God about spiritual battles being faced by people in your church. Pray for your pastor and other church leaders. Ask the Lord to protect them, strengthen them, and give them boldness to accomplish all He desires through them.

Day 4 • The Power of the Tongue

Read and meditate on "God's Word for Today" and "Today's Spiritual Reality" in the margin. Begin today's study with prayer.

God's Word for Today

"With [the tongue] we bless our Lord and Father, and with it we curse men who are made in God's likeness. Out of the same mouth come blessing and cursing. My brothers, these things should not be this way." James 3:9–10

Today's Spiritual Reality

Our words either build up or tear down those in the body of Christ.

It can be argued that the tongue is the most powerful part of the human body. With our words we can either encourage others or tear them down. James marveled at the discrepancy of our words. He witnessed those in the early church blessing God one minute and cursing others the next. He then proclaimed, "These things should not be this way" (James 3:10).

Unfortunately, James would most likely encounter this same problem in our churches today. We too fail to realize the power of our words. It is easy to criticize or attack others in our church family, especially when they mess up. We must realize that God is the one who gave us the power of communication, and He intends that we use it to build up His body.

(1) **Mark the following statements *T* for *true* or *F* for *false*.**

__ 1. God intends for us to use our words to build up His body.

__ 2. Our words can hurt and tear others down.

(2) **Mark each of the following uses of the tongue as either one that *(B)* builds up the body or *(H)* hurts and tears down the body.**

___ Slander	___ Encourage	___ Pray
___ Unjustly criticize	___ Lie	___ Gossip
___ Teach	___ Counsel	___ Prophesy
___ Loving correction	___ Belittle	___ Curse
___ Praise	___ Witness about Christ	___ Sing hymns
___ Tell dirty jokes	___ Defame	___ Slur
___ Discourage	___ Malign	___ Libel
___ Preach	___ Dis	___ Smear
___ Admonish	___ Inspire	___ Incite

If we could see our lives from the Lord's perspective, we would better understand the power of our words to either soothe or sting. The tongue is powerful, but with the Lord's help it can and should be harnessed for His glory. When this happens, our words become helpful and encouraging to those in our church family. With our words we can help others bear their burdens.

#1 answers: 1-T, 2-T

Many times a brother or a sister in Christ has encouraged me (Bo). They may have dropped by for a visit, called, e-mailed, or sent me a card. Their words of encouragement often came at times when the burden seemed heavy. As I listened to them, the burden seemed lighter because I felt encouraged in the Lord. I keep those cards and e-mails in a special file. When times get difficult, I reread them and again find encouragement.

Even though the tongue is a great gift from God that He intends for His glory, we can choose to use it for our own selfish gain. When this is our attitude, our words harm those in the body of Christ. Instead of using our words to help carry the burdens of others, we actually add to the burdens and hurts of our fellow believers.

The Lord has given me opportunities to minister to several churches in crisis. I never cease to be amazed by the depth of pain that has been caused by words. The hurt is often carried for years. In some cases the painful memories even drive people away from the church. We must ask the Lord to help us use our words to build up His body instead of damage it.

Some people who hurt others use the excuse that they are just being truthful, and it is not their fault the person was hurt. We should speak the truth to one another, but not all truth needs to be shared if it would damage the body. When we share the truth, Ephesians 4:15 makes clear that we must do so in love. God's love is to be the guiding force in all we do and say.

Not all truth needs to be shared if it would damage the body.

Ephesians 4:15
"Speak the truth in love."

3 **How are you using your words in relation to those in your church?**
○ a. I am seeking to build up and encourage those in my church family.
○ b. Sometimes my words build up, and sometimes they tear down.
○ c. My words often hurt others and tear down the body of Christ.

If we bore the burdens of others by building them up with encouraging words, our churches would experience healing, comfort, and blessing. Will you ask the Lord to help you become a person whose words bring peace, encouragement, and hope to those in His body?

Conclude today's lesson by talking with God about uses of the tongue in your church. Pray that God will transform members whose words hurt and tear down others. Ask God to increase the number of people who build up the body with their words.

Day 5 • Keeping the Unity of the Spirit

God's Word for Today

"You are no longer foreigners and strangers, but fellow citizens with the saints, and members of God's household." Ephesians 2:19

Today's Spiritual Reality

God wants unity, not uniformity, in the church.

Read and meditate on "God's Word for Today" and "Today's Spiritual Reality" in the margin. Begin today's study with prayer.

Bearing one another's burdens requires accepting the fact that God has built His church with people who are very different. The early church was also made up of people from different social, ethnic, and religious backgrounds. The one essential element that united the church was believers' common life in Christ. Because all had been born again, background didn't matter. But they still had to learn how to function together and care for one another.

A difference in backgrounds often brings differences of opinion. These differences challenge a church body, but they shouldn't divide it. In Christ we are the same—sinners saved by grace. In the midst of these differences we can find opportunities to bear one another's burdens.

1. **What unites us as a church made up of different people? Check one.**

○ a. Common country
○ b. Common life in Christ
○ c. Common ideas
○ d. Common interests

A few years ago the Lord led our church to sponsor a refugee couple. This couple came from a country where they had suffered great persecution. After months of praying and working, they were finally allowed to come to Canada. When they arrived, our church family rallied around them and helped bear the burden of adapting to a new life. Soon both of them accepted Christ, were baptized, and began to grow in Christ. As great as that sounds, it still wasn't easy. They struggled with the language and culture. But the church showed them grace and loved them. We were different, but in Christ we were unified as family.

Unity means even though we may have differences, we are of one heart and mind in following Christ.

There is a big difference between uniformity and unity in the church. Uniformity means everyone must think alike and approach things the same way. Unity means even though we may have differences, we are of one heart and mind in following Christ. God calls us to unity, not uniformity. This means the diversity of members within the body will result in a variety of views and expectations. Instead of being a weakness, differences are actually a strength in the body of Christ.

#1 answer: b

(2) **Match the definitions on the right with the terms on the left.**

__ 1. Unity a. Everyone must be alike in thinking and approach.

__ 2. Uniformity b. Different but together in seeking to follow Christ

In the presence of a variety of people and backgrounds, we can most clearly demonstrate the love of God and the change He has brought in our lives. The early church had a conflict because of differences among its members. In Acts 6:1 we read that "there arose a complaint" in the church because one ethnic group of widows was being overlooked. The church did not quarrel and divide but sought to bear the burdens of those being overlooked. The apostles understood the importance of the church's unity. A church always has differences, but it does everything possible to remain united in Christ.

Ephesians 4:1-3

"I, therefore, the prisoner in the Lord, urge you to walk worthy of the calling you have received, with all humility and gentleness, with patience, accepting one another in love, diligently keeping the unity of the Spirit with the peace that binds us."

(3) **Read Ephesians 4:1-3 in the margin and circle words that describe attitudes and behaviors that contribute to keeping unity in the body.**

Humility, gentleness, patience, acceptance, and love all contribute to keeping the unity of the Spirit. To bear the burdens of others within a context of differences requires one foundational principle: putting others above yourself. Philippians 2:3-4 states, "Do nothing out of rivalry or conceit, but in humility consider others as more important than yourselves. Everyone should look out not only for his own interests, but also for the interests of others." Paul knew self-centered people would cause the church body to quickly divide and become immobilized. But if members of the body placed the interests of others above their own, the Lord could do anything through them. We place others above ourselves by attentively looking for opportunities to carry one another's burdens.

#2 answer: unity–b, uniformity–a

#4 answer: c

(4) **What is the foundational principle for bearing one another's burdens?**

○ a. Put yourself first.
○ b. Ignore others.
○ c. Put others above yourself.
○ d. Look out for yourself.

Responding to the Lord

Review this week's lessons and underline the statement or Scripture God seemed to emphasize to you the most. Ask the Lord to show you how He wants you to respond to Him and to His people in light of what He has said to you this week. Write in the margin a prayer of response to the Lord. Then review your prayer responses in day 5 for each week in our study. Thank God for what He has taught you and what He has done in your life and in your small group.

Session 6 • Bearing One Another's Burdens

Use some or all of the following suggestions to guide your small-group experience this week.

Opening Prayer

Building Relationships

Share the following with your group.

1. In what way have you experienced fellowship with believers most during the past six weeks?
2. What have you done in response to this study (either toward God or others) that has been the most meaningful to you?

Responding to Learning Activities

1. Share your responses to some or all of the following learning activities.
   - Page 83, activity 2
   - Page 85, activity 3
   - Page 87, activity 3. Why?
   - Page 88, activity 2. Compare your responses.
2. Divide into smaller, same-gender groups of four persons each (men with men, women with women). Share your responses to activities 3–4 on page 83 and activity 2 on page 87. Ask one person at a time, *How can we pray for you?* Then take time to pray for each person.

Reviewing Week 6

1. In pairs or triads take turns reciting your Scripture-memory verse, Galatians 6:2.
2. Review this week's daily spiritual realities, reproduced below. Which one do you think identifies a reality you and your church most need to develop more fully so that you will experience God's best as a fellowship of believers? Why?
   - Day 1: Because we live in a fallen world, we need one another.
   - Day 2: We need to help carry one another's physical burdens.
   - Day 3: We need to help carry one another's spiritual burdens.
   - Day 4: Our words either build up or tear down those in the body of Christ.
   - Day 5: God wants unity, not uniformity, in the church.

3. Identify some common burdens in your church. How could you or your small group help bear such burdens?
4. Describe the impacts, positive and negative, that our words have on the body of Christ.
5. What is the difference between unity and uniformity? Which quality does God's Spirit produce in the church? What are some ways we can help maintain it (day 5 and p. 91, activities 2–4)?

Building Up the Body

1. During your review at the end of day 5, what statement or Scripture did you identify that you think God emphasized most this week?
2. Which truth that you have studied this week do you think would do the most to build up the body of Christ if you and other members of your church faithfully applied it?
3. How do you want to respond to what you have learned this week? How has the Lord prompted you this week to love His people and build up His body?

Praying Together

Close your study by praying conversationally—brief prayers on a variety of subjects about which members may pray multiple times. Pray about one subject at a time. Pray that you and your church will be a healthy body of Christ that loves one another and brings glory to Christ, your head.

Planning for Your Next Discipleship Study

Leader: If you are offering another study in the Growing Disciples Series, make books available so that members can begin preparing for the first session. If not, announce other upcoming opportunities for discipleship.

Are You in the Family?

Are you a member of God's family? Paul wrote to the Corinthians, "Examine yourselves to see whether you are in the faith; test yourselves. Do you not realize that Christ Jesus is in you—unless, of course, you fail the test?" (2 Corinthians 13:5, NIV). How would you know for sure whether you are "in the faith"? Paul said you would know by the Spirit of Jesus Christ who is in you. Other Scriptures describe how you can know. When God's Spirit is in you, your life will bear spiritual fruit.

1. **Read the following Scriptures and underline the words that describe ways a person can know he or she is "in the faith." I've underlined the first one for you.**

   Romans 8:16—"<u>The Spirit Himself testifies together with our spirit</u> that we are God's children."

   1 John 2:3-6—"This is how we are sure that we have come to know Him: by keeping His commands. The one who says, 'I have come to know Him,' without keeping His commands, is a liar, and the truth is not in him. But whoever keeps His word, truly in him the love of God is perfected. This is how we know we are in Him: the one who says he remains in Him should walk just as He walked."

   1 John 3:24—"The one who keeps His commands remains in Him, and He in him. And the way we know that He remains in us is from the Spirit He has given us."

   1 John 4:13—"This is how we know that we remain in Him and He in us: He has given to us from His Spirit."

The Holy Spirit testifies, or bears witness, to your spirit that you belong to God. The presence and work of the Holy Spirit in you can help you know you are God's child. John says you can know you are in Him if you obey His commands.

2. **Does the Holy Spirit bear witness to you that you are a child of God?**
   - ○ Yes
   - ○ No
   - ○ I don't know for sure.

3. **Do you obey Christ and walk as Jesus walked in such a way that you know the Spirit of Christ dwells in you?**
   - ○ Yes
   - ○ No
   - ○ My inconsistency raises questions for me.

Read the following list of the fruit of the Spirit. Ask God to reveal to you whether His Spirit lives in you and bears this kind of fruit in and through your life.

Galatians 5:22-23—"The fruit of the Spirit is love, joy, peace, patience, kindness, goodness, faith, gentleness, self-control."

4. **If God judged your life by the evidence of His Spirit's fruit in your life, what do you think He would conclude? Check one or write your own response.**
   - ○ a. I don't see any evidence of the Spirit's fruit.
   - ○ b. The Spirit is present, but the fruit is very immature.
   - ○ c. The Spirit is clearly evident by the quality and quantity of fruit I see.
   - ○ d. Other: ____________________

   ____

   ____

   ____

5. **Have you placed your faith and trust in Jesus Christ alone for your salvation?**
   - ○ Yes
   - ○ No

6. **As you have placed yourself before God seeking to know whether you are His child—whether you are in His family—what do you sense His Spirit has revealed to you? Check the choice that best describes your condition.**
   - ○ a. Jesus is in me. I know it by the witness of His Spirit and the evidence of His fruit in me.
   - ○ b. My life in Christ is very weak, but Jesus is in me.
   - ○ c. His Spirit is not in me. I am still without Christ.
   - ○ d. I am still not sure which of these conditions is true of me.

If you still are not sure about your condition before God *(d)*, continue to seek His counsel in the days to come. This is an important issue that is worth your time and effort. God wants to know you more than you desire it, so continue to seek Him. If doubt persists, go ahead and settle your relationship with Him in faith. If you realize that you do not have a saving relationship with Christ *(c)*, move to "Born Again" on the following page or ask a pastor, your small-group leader, or another believer to help you receive Christ as your Savior.

7. **If you have that relationship with Jesus Christ, take a moment to reflect on the time when you entered that saving relationship with Him. Write some of your memories of that time.**

   ____

   ____

   ____

   ____

   ____

   ____

   ____

   ____

Adapted from Claude King, *Come to the Lord's Table* (Nashville: LifeWay Press, 2006), 40–44. Used by permission.

Born Again

You may wonder what is meant by the term *new birth* that was used in week 1 of this study. Jesus said in John 3:3 that "unless someone is born again, he cannot see the kingdom of God." Just as we have been born physically, we must also be born spiritually.

You need to be born again because of the eternal consequences of your sin. Romans 6:23 states that "the wages of sin is death, but the gift of God is eternal life in Christ Jesus our Lord." Because of sin each of us is destined to perish eternally. Jesus came from heaven to be the sacrifice for your sin and to become the way to an eternal love relationship with God.

John 3:16 states, "God loved the world in this way: He gave His One and Only Son, so that everyone who believes in Him will not perish but have eternal life." Now because of Jesus you have a way to God. Yet there is still a condition to your receiving salvation and eternal life: you must believe.

The belief that Jesus was talking about is the key to your being born again. To believe in Jesus is more than simply agreeing that He is the Son of God. It is to make a deliberate decision to trust Him as your personal Savior and Lord. You do this by talking to God in prayer. You confess to Jesus that you are a sinner and that you believe He died and rose again to save you and give you eternal life. You repent, or turn away, from your sin and choose to live life His way.

It is in this simple prayer and act of faith that God causes you to be born again as His child. You now have the opportunity to live in a deep, growing relationship with God.

But one thing that must not be overlooked in God's rebirth process is the fact that He causes you to be born again into His family. You aren't to live your life independent of your brothers and sisters in Christ. You are to live this life in fellowship together with God's family, united in Christ. This is why being part of a local church is so vital.

If you have yet to ask Jesus into your life, consider stopping at this point and praying the prayer below.

> Lord Jesus, I know I am a sinner and do not deserve eternal life. But I believe You died and rose from the grave to save me and cause me to be born again as a child of God. Jesus, please forgive my sins and save me. Come into my life and take control of my life. I now place my trust in You alone for my salvation, and I accept Your free gift of eternal life.

Share your decision with a brother or sister in Christ. Also ask the Lord to direct you to the church family He wants you to join.

My Place in His Body

It's great when people begin to realize that God has shaped them to function as members of His body, their church. Usually, the next question they ask is "How do I know my place in His body?" This is a legitimate question.

First, recognize that the Lord shaped you and placed you in your church, so He is the only One who can guide you to know where He wants you to fit. Your natural tendency is to ask someone else to show you. But the Lord wants to draw you closer in your relationship with Him. Therefore, He wants you to seek Him and His purpose.

God has given you the way to seek Him-through prayer. You must spend time with Him in prayer. But don't pray just to find out things you want to know. Spend time with your Lord because you love Him and want to know Him more. As you seek Him in prayer, He shapes your life and unfolds His purpose.

God has also given you His Spirit, who works in your life to guide you. God wants you to know what He desires and how you can obey Him. Therefore, you need to ask Him to show you what He is doing in your church. How is He shaping and forming your church to accomplish His purpose? Also ask the Lord to reveal to you what He had in mind when He added you to your church.

It may take time for the Lord to reveal your place in His body. Be patient and allow Him to shape your life.

You may not know whether you are a knee or an arm in the body, but that doesn't mean you have to sit by idly. Jesus has already commanded you to love one another just as He loves you (see John 13:34); so you don't have to hold back, waiting for Him to tell you to love your church family. You can begin looking for ways the Lord wants you to show His love toward those in your church family. Go for it!

A word of caution: don't assume the Lord wants you to serve only in the ways you are most comfortable. He may want you to serve in those ways, but don't limit Him. As the Lord of your life, He will often cause you to trust Him in deeper ways by stretching you.

Another word of caution: never bypass your relationship with Christ in order to do His assignments. The assignments must flow from your love relationship with Him. When they don't, the Lord isn't happy, and you must repent (see Revelation 2:1-5).

Pray and thank the Lord for shaping you as He desired and for placing you in your church family. Release your life to Him to use in whatever way He wants to build up His body. Ask Him to guide you to a place of meaningful service to His body.

For more help on finding your place in the body, see Henry Blackaby and Mel Blackaby, *What's So Spiritual About Your Gifts?* (Sisters, OR: Multnomah, 2004).

Instructions for the Body of Christ in Romans 12:9-21

① **Read Romans 12:9-21 below and watch for ways Paul instructs believers to treat one another in the body of Christ.**

9“Love must be without hypoc-
risy. Detest evil; cling to what is
good. 10Show family affection to one
another with brotherly love. Outdo
one another in showing honor. 11Do
not lack diligence; be fervent in spirit;
serve the Lord. 12Rejoice in hope; be
patient in affliction; be persistent in
prayer. 13Share with the saints in their
needs; pursue hospitality. 14Bless those
who persecute you; bless and do not
curse. 15Rejoice with those who rejoice;
weep with those who weep. 16Be in
agreement with one another. Do not
be proud; instead, associate with the
humble. Do not be wise in your own
estimation. 17Do not repay anyone evil
for evil. Try to do what is honorable
in everyone’s eyes. 18If possible, on
your part, live at peace with everyone.
19Friends, do not avenge yourselves;
instead, leave room for His wrath. For
it is written: ‘Vengeance belongs to
Me; I will repay,’ says the Lord.

20“But
‘If your enemy is hungry, feed him.
If he is thirsty, give him something
to drink.
For in so doing you will be heaping
fiery coals on his head.’

21Do not be conquered by evil, but
conquer evil with good.”

② **Which of the many instructions given in these verses do you think you need to practice more than you do? Underline them below. Which ones do members of your church need to practice more than they do? Check the top five.[1]**

- ○ Love others sincerely.
- ○ Bless those who persecute you.
- ○ Hate evil.
- ○ Rejoice with those who rejoice.
- ○ Cling to what is good.
- ○ Mourn with those who mourn.
- ○ Be devoted to one another.
- ○ Live in harmony with one another.
- ○ Honor one another.
- ○ Don’t be proud or conceited.
- ○ Serve the Lord with zeal.
- ○ Associate with people of low position.
- ○ Be joyful in hope.
- ○ Don’t repay evil for evil.
- ○ Be patient in affliction.
- ○ Do what is right.
- ○ Be faithful in prayer.
- ○ Don’t take revenge.
- ○ Share with God’s people in need.
- ○ Overcome evil with good.
- ○ Practice hospitality.

1. Adapted from Henry Blackaby, Richard Blackaby, and Claude King, *Experiencing God* (Nashville: LifeWay Press, 2007), 210. Used by permission.

Review the list of instructions from Romans 12:9-21. Pray and ask the Lord what specific actions He wants you to take to apply these instructions in your relationships in your church. Write notes below about the things you sense God wants you to do.

"One Anothers" for the Body of Christ

The body of Christ is an important place to demonstrate our *koinonia* with God as we live in fellowship with others. Many Scripture passages instruct us in how to relate to one another. Use the following list to evaluate your own relationships. Read the related Scriptures for additional insights. Watch for opportunities to apply these instructions in your relationships.

(The words *one another* have been italicized in the following Scriptures for emphasis.)

• Accept one another.

"Accept *one another*, just as the Messiah also accepted you, to the glory of God" (Romans 15:7).

• Be at peace with one another.

"Salt is good, but if the salt should lose its flavor, how can you make it salty? Have salt among yourselves and be at peace with *one another*" (Mark 9:50).

• Be hospitable to one another.

"Be hospitable to *one another* without complaining" (1 Peter 4:9).

• Be in agreement with one another.

"Be in agreement with *one another*. Do not be proud; instead, associate with the humble. Do not be wise in your own estimation" (Romans 12:16).

• Be kind and compassionate to one another.

"Be kind and compassionate to *one another*, forgiving *one another*, just as God also forgave you in Christ" (Ephesians 4:32).

• Forgive one another.

"Put on heartfelt compassion, kindness, humility, gentleness, and patience, accepting *one another* and forgiving *one another* if anyone has a complaint against another. Just as the Lord has forgiven you, so also you must forgive" (Colossians 3:12-13).

• Bear with one another.

"Live a life worthy of the calling you have received. Be completely humble and gentle; be patient, bearing with *one another* in love" (Ephesians 4:1-2, NIV).

• Build each other up and encourage one another.

"Encourage *one another* and build each other up as you are already doing" (1 Thessalonians 5:11).

• Clothe yourselves with humility toward one another.

"Clothe yourselves with humility toward *one another*, because 'God resists the proud, but gives grace to the humble' " (1 Peter 5:5).

- **Confess your sins to one another and pray for one another.**

"Confess your sins to *one another* and pray for *one another*, so that you may be healed. The intense prayer of the righteous is very powerful" (James 5:16).

- **Love one another.**

"I give you a new commandment: love *one another*. Just as I have loved you, you must also love *one another*" (John 13:34).

"Do not owe anyone anything, except to love *one another*, for the one who loves another has fulfilled the law" (Romans 13:8).

"By obedience to the truth, having purified yourselves for sincere love of the brothers, love *one another* earnestly from a pure heart" (1 Peter 1:22).

"This is His command: that we believe in the name of His Son Jesus Christ, and love *one another* as He commanded us" (1 John 3:23).

"Dear friends, let us love *one another*, because love is from God, and everyone who loves has been born of God and knows God" (1 John 4:7).

- **Pursue what is good for one another.**

"See to it that no one repays evil for evil to anyone, but always pursue what is good for *one another* and for all" (1 Thessalonians 5:15).

- **Serve one another.**

"Serve *one another* through love" (Galatians 5:13).

- **Show family affection to one another and show honor to one another.**

"Show family affection to *one another* with brotherly love. Outdo *one another* in showing honor" (Romans 12:10).

- **Speak to one another and submit to one another.**

"Be filled with the Spirit: speaking to *one another* in psalms, hymns, and spiritual songs, singing and making music to the Lord in your heart, giving thanks always for everything to God the Father in the name of our Lord Jesus Christ, submitting to *one another* in the fear of Christ" (Ephesians 5:18-21).

- **Spur one another on.**

"Let us consider how we may spur *one another* on toward love and good deeds" (Hebrews 10:24, NIV).

- **Teach and admonish one another.**

"Let the message about the Messiah dwell richly among you, teaching and admonishing *one another* in all wisdom" (Colossians 3:16).

Pray and ask God to enable you to consistently apply these actions in your relationships with others in the body of Christ.

The Love Test

Jesus commands us to love one another just as He loves us. This can be a daunting assignment when we consider how He has loved us. Yet we must remember that He will never ask us to do something He will not equip us for and help us do.

A church should overflow with the love of Christ. This occurs when we obey His command and express His love to one another. Paul gave us a very clear picture of this ideal when he described love in 1 Corinthians 13. In this chapter Paul first pointed out that if something is done without God's love, it is worthless. He then described to the church in Corinth what love looks like.

1. **Read the following verses from 1 Corinthians 13. Then answer the questions to indicate how you exhibit love in these ways toward those in your church.**

> "Love is patient; love is kind. Love does not envy; is not boastful; is not conceited; does not act improperly; is not selfish; is not provoked; does not keep a record of wrongs; finds no joy in unrighteousness, but rejoices in the truth; bears all things, believes all things, hopes all things, endures all things. Love never ends" (1 Corinthians 13:4-8).

1. I am patient with those in my church.
   ○ False ○ Occasionally ○ True

2. I am kind to those in my church.
   ○ False ○ Occasionally ○ True

3. I do not envy those in my church family.
   ○ False ○ Occasionally ○ True

4. I do not focus on myself and boast or act selfishly when relating to others.
   ○ False ○ Occasionally ○ True

5. I do not get angry with my church family.
○ False ○ Occasionally ○ True

6. I do not hold grudges toward those in my church who have wronged me.
○ False ○ Occasionally ○ True

7. I protect those in my church family.
○ False ○ Occasionally ○ True

8. I trust those in my church family.
○ False ○ Occasionally ○ True

9. I think the best about those in my church.
○ False ○ Occasionally ○ True

10. I am committed to my church family.
○ False ○ Occasionally ○ True

11. I do not fail those in my church family.
○ False ○ Occasionally ○ True

(2) **Review the list of ways you should demonstrate love toward others. In the space below each item, write specific actions you can take to correct wrong behavior or to demonstrate love toward a specific person or group. Write their names as well.**

Spend time with the Lord in prayer. Ask Him to teach you how to love as described in these verses and ask Him to give you a heart to love others in these ways.

A Love Feast (Agape Meal)

The New Testament indicates that the churches had a mealtime they called a love feast or *agape* (Greek word for *love)* meal. We don't know exactly what took place at these meals, but they were more than an observance of the Lord's Supper. Some groups in history have experienced wonderful Christian fellowship and love at times they called a love feast.

The following suggestions are for an optional activity your group or church might consider to enjoy your covenant relationship with one another. If you decide to conduct a love feast, take time to plan for a meaningful experience together. Consider the following ideas and suggestions in planning your meal. Keep in mind that Scripture does not give instructions for the love feast beyond its instructions for the Lord's Supper. Don't feel restricted by these suggestions. Enjoy yourselves as you express your love to one another.

THE MEAL

The meal can be simple or complex. Moravians serve a sweet bun and a cup of coffee for their love feasts. You could have a more extensive meal, a potluck meal, or a full-blown dinner on the grounds. One key to keep in mind is that the fellowship is to be the emphasis, not the food. Don't just eat and leave.

SINGING

The service should be light and more spontaneous than structured. Consider conducting a hymn sing featuring requests, favorites, or songs that focus on love for Christ and on unity and Christian love for one another.

TESTIMONIES

Invite testimonies on what God has done in your church body that has been particularly meaningful. Start by asking members to share testimonies around their tables or in small groups of about eight. These should be voluntary, so don't go around the circle. Testimonies could include answered prayers, revival experiences, special events at which lives were changed, special victories when faced with challenges, victories over sin, relationships reconciled, deeper experiences of Christ's love, experiences of the Heavenly Father's love, special experiences at a Lord's Supper or baptism service, experiences of God's love through other members of the body, God's provision in a time of need, and so forth. After members have shared in small groups, call for testimonies to be shared with the large group.

AFFIRMATIONS

Too often we fail to say thank you or to affirm what God is doing in and through those around us. Provide an opportunity for public thank-you's or for affirming blessings in the lives of others. Invite people to finish this sentence: "I thank God for [name] because. …" You might even recognize some groups of people for a group thank-you, such as teachers, workers with preschoolers, ushers, or others who may seldom receive thanks for their ministry to the body. Think of other ways for members to express love and appreciation for members of the body of Christ.

LOVE OFFERING

Consider receiving a love offering as an expression of gratitude to Christ for what He has done. If you decide to receive a love offering, announce the opportunity early in the study so that people will have time to reflect, pray, and prepare. Invite members to consider giving a special love offering above their regular giving to express an extra thank-you to Christ for His love and sacrifice. Decide in advance how you will use this special offering. You might use it for church members' benevolent needs, as the church in Acts did with gifts like that of Barnabas in Acts 4:32-37. You might use it for a special mission project. You might give it to a church on the mission field or to a needy church in your own city.

If you are willing to manage the process, the offerings could be more than money. People might choose to give other things of value for use by others in the body of Christ or things that could be sold, such as jewelry, used cars, stocks, volunteer service for a particular project, and so on. You might even suggest that people consider bring idols of the heart (something that has captured the heart so that a person doesn't love the Lord with a whole heart) to give away. This offering could include a boat, a collection, toys, material things that have captured their love, and so forth.

Let this offering be a matter of joy, not obligation. Encourage people to have fun deciding what to give and to have joy in blessing others as they use the gifts to show God's love to one another.

PRAYERS

Invite volunteers to stand and pray prayers of thanksgiving, praise, adoration, and love to Christ for His love and for the love the body of Christ has demonstrated to one another.

Adapted from Claude King, *Come to the Lord's Table* (Nashville: LifeWay Press, 2006), 123–24. Used by permission.

If you have not read the introduction beginning on page 6, do so before continuing.

MAKING DISCIPLES

Jesus gave a final command to His followers: "Go, therefore, and make disciples of all nations, … teaching them to observe everything I have commanded you" (Matthew 28:19-20). As people come to faith in Christ, we have the task of teaching them obedience to all He commanded. This is a huge assignment that we must take seriously. Leading a small-group study of *Growing Disciples: Fellowship with Believers* is one way you can obey the final command. Our goal is to help new and growing believers in Jesus Christ develop a balanced, well-rounded spiritual life. We will do that by helping them understand how to experience God's best in fellowship with other believers in the body of Christ.

God's intent is not that His children live in isolation but that they join their lives together with their brothers and sisters in Christ. This is why He has given us the local church and placed it in the world to function as His body. As members of His body, we each have a God-given function to play. As we seek to function together as His body, God accomplishes His eternal purpose through our lives and His church.

Many Christians do not seem to understand the importance of their connection not only with Christ but also with one another. Leading a small-group study of *Fellowship with Believers* is one way you can help God's people begin to make the necessary adjustments so that they can begin to function together as the body of Christ.

SELECTING A LEADER

If you are not the person who plans to lead this study, enlist a mature believer to lead the group. Select a leader who has a warm, personal, and faithful walk with Christ. Look for good interpersonal skills and the ability to facilitate small-group learning activities.

SMALL-GROUP STUDY

This resource has been designed for a combination of individual and small-group study. In a small group of other believers, Christians can learn from one another, encourage and strengthen one another, and minister to one another. The body of Christ can function best as members assume responsibility for helping one another grow in Christlikeness. Encourage participants to study the member book during the week and then join other believers in the small group to process and apply what they have learned. Provide a separate group for every 8 to 12 participants so that everyone will be able to participate actively.

ONE-TO-ONE MENTORING

If circumstances prevent your studying in a small-group setting in which you have access to a variety of gifts, you may choose to use the book in a one-to-one mentoring or coaching process. To do so, study the devotionals each day and meet at least once each week to discuss what you are learning. Use the session plans at the end of each week's devotionals to get ideas for your personal discussions and prayer time. Pray for and encourage each other by phone.

ENLISTING PARTICIPANTS

Any believer who desires to know Christ more and to function as He desires will benefit from this study. As you enlist participants, give members a book before the first session and ask them to study the introduction and week 1 prior to the session. Include mature believers in the group so that each subgroup will include someone who will be comfortable praying for the others and can lead in discussion when needed.

YOUR ROLE AS THE LEADER

You are not required to be a content expert to teach this course. Participants study the content during the week. Your role is to facilitate group discussion, share, and pray to process and apply what participants have learned during the week. Be sensitive to the growth of members and pay special attention to those who may struggle along the way. Don't hesitate to enlist the help of more mature believers in the group to help you nurture the others. Always remember that your job as the leader is to continually point people to Christ and their relationship with Him. You can depend on other members of the body to help you as your group seeks the Lord together.

TIME AND SCHEDULE

This course is designed for six sessions. The group sessions need to follow the study of the week's daily devotionals. Members will need to have books so that they can study the first week's material prior to the first session. If you are not able to distribute books before the first session, use that session to distribute books and get to know one another. This will add one additional session to the study. Allow at least 60 minutes—preferably 90—for the session. The longer session will provide adequate time for personal sharing, discussion, and prayer for one another.

OPTIONAL INTRODUCTORY RETREAT

If you want to jump-start the experience of biblical fellowship *(koinonia)*, conduct a retreat to start the study. Use the content of the first week and the first group session to conduct the retreat. Spend time getting acquainted. Plan for times of fellowship around meals and recreation. Provide quiet times for individuals to study the individual lessons and come together to process the lessons two or three times during the retreat. Include personal testimonies from those who have followed Christ for a while.

PREPARING FOR THE STUDY

The most important thing you can do to prepare for the study each week is to allow the Lord to prepare you and fill you with His Spirit. So make prayer a major part of your preparation throughout the course. God will work and guide in answer to prayer. Leading the small-group sessions should not require large amounts of time in advance preparation. Each week study the suggestions that follow the week's devotionals. Use these as options for leading the session, not as a rigid structure to follow. The Lord will put each group together in a unique way. Therefore, allow the needs of your group to dictate the emphasis you give to each topic. Decide which activities and questions to use in your study and determine approximate times for transitions between segments. Select activities that are most appropriate for your group's maturity level.

DURING THE SESSION

1. *Prayer.* Some believers are uncomfortable praying aloud in a group. However, it is crucial that the body pray together and for one another. Begin by asking for volunteers. Don't call on people to pray unless you know they can do so comfortably. Give permission for people not to pray aloud until they are ready. Seek to increase their prayer participation as the study progresses.
2. *Opening prayer.* Start each group time with prayer. Prayer is not simply a spiritual discipline; it is our very life as children of God and His church. Make this a significant time. It may be helpful to begin with a time of silence to allow the group to focus their minds and hearts on the Lord. Then you or someone in the group can voice a prayer asking for the Spirit's guidance during your time together.
3. *Building relationships.* These activities are more surface, get-acquainted topics that grow deeper as the weeks go by. Adjust the sharing if your group is already well acquainted.
4. *Responding to learning activities.* Model sharing, based on your own responses. Give several people or all an opportunity to share their responses.
5. *Reviewing this week's material.* These activities help you review the facts or key ideas.
6. *Building up the body.* Invite responses to these questions and activities. Watch for ways to encourage one another as you seek to build up the body of Christ.
7. *Praying together.* Corporate prayer is often missing in our Christian lives. Encourage your group to begin praying together. Watch for opportunities to pause and pray as a group for needs of specific members.
8. *Previewing next week.* Use the introductory page to give a quick overview of the upcoming week's study. You could invite volunteers to prepare in advance to introduce the next week's topic.

This guide may help you lead your group, but the Holy Spirit is your true Guide. Allow Him to show you what questions to ask and the direction He wants the group to go each week.

OPTIONAL LOVE FEAST

Consider the suggestions for a love feast in the Discipleship Helps section on pages 104–5 as a concluding celebration for your study.

Your Church Experiencing God Together

You have started the journey of experiencing God together with your church as the body of Christ. This study has been an introduction for you and your church.

Are you ready to go deeper?

Mel has written another course on the church with his father, Henry Blackaby, the coauthor of *Experiencing God: Knowing and Doing the Will of God. Your Church Experiencing God Together* can be a valuable next step in helping your church mature as the body of Christ.

Henry Blackaby calls this book a necessary sequel to *Experiencing God.* It challenges Christians to transition from knowing and doing the will of God as individuals to knowing and doing the will of God within a corporate body of believers. *Experiencing God* helps people get on track with God. *Your Church Experiencing God Together* guides their journey within the family of God.

This nine-session, video-enhanced study is filled with engaging stories from both Henry's and Mel's pastoral experiences. Some Christians feel they can worship just as well outside the church walls; others feel no need to be more than spectators or consumer Christians. *Your Church Experiencing God Together* affirms God's plan for all believers to utilize their spiritual gifts as part of a loving, covenant church body under Christ's headship, empowered by the Holy Spirit to impact a watching world.

The leader kit includes the member book with a leader guide at the back and five videotapes, including an introductory session and eight group sessions featuring the beautiful Canadian Rockies, Henry and Mel in a seminar setting, and documentary interviews with members of Bow Valley Baptist Church.

Member Book (001203266)
Leader Kit (001203268)

To order these resources and to check availability, fax (615) 251-5933; phone toll free (800) 458-2772; order online at *www.lifeway.com;* e-mail *orderentry@lifeway.com;* visit the LifeWay Christian Store serving you; or write to LifeWay Church Resources Customer Service; One LifeWay Plaza; Nashville, TN 37234-0113.

The Growing Disciples Series

New and growing believers need a firm foundation on which to build their lives. The Growing Disciples Series provides short-term Bible studies that establish a strong foundation for a life of following Jesus Christ. The series begins with *The Call to Follow Christ,* which introduces six spiritual disciplines. Subsequent studies help believers understand and practice disciplines that strengthen their love relationship with Christ and develop a lifestyle of faithful, fruitful obedience. Watch for the following six-week resources as the series grows:

Growing Disciples: Abide in Christ
Growing Disciples: Live in the Word
Growing Disciples: Pray in Faith
Growing Disciples: Fellowship with Believers
Growing Disciples: Witness to the World
Growing Disciples: Minister to Others

For a free 20-minute Webinar on the series, go to *http://lifeway.acrobat.com/growingdisciples*.

The Call to Follow Christ: Six Disciplines for New and Growing Believers by Claude King is a seven-session, foundational resource that introduces the six disciplines in the series. This unique workbook includes a music CD with seven songs sung by Dámaris Carbaugh that will enrich participants' daily 10- to 15-minute interactive devotion/study time. Item 001303666

To order these resources and to check availability, fax (615) 251-5933; phone toll free (800) 458-2772; order online at *www.lifeway.com;* e-mail *orderentry@lifeway.com;* visit the LifeWay Christian Store serving you; or write to LifeWay Church Resources Customer Service; One LifeWay Plaza; Nashville, TN 37234-0113.

CHRISTIAN GROWTH STUDY PLAN

In the Christian Growth Study Plan *Growing Disciples: Fellowship with Believers* is a resource for course credit in the subject area The Church in the Christian Growth category of diploma plans. To receive credit, read the book; complete the learning activities; attend group sessions; show your work to your pastor, a staff member, or a church leader; then complete the form. This page may be duplicated. Send the completed form to:

Christian Growth Study Plan; One LifeWay Plaza; Nashville, TN 37234-0117
Fax (615) 251-5067; e-mail *cgspnet@lifeway.com*

For information about the Christian Growth Study Plan, refer to the current Christian Growth Study Plan Catalog, located online at *www.lifeway.com/cgsp*. If you do not have access to the Internet, contact the Christian Growth Study Plan office, (800) 968-5519, for the specific plan you need.

Fellowship with Believers
COURSE NUMBER: CG-1257

PARTICIPANT INFORMATION

Social Security Number (USA ONLY-optional)	Personal CGSP Number*	Date of Birth (MONTH, DAY, YEAR)
- -	- -	- -

Name (First, Middle, Last)	Home Phone
	- -

Address (Street, Route, or P.O. Box)	City, State, or Province	Zip/Postal Code

Email Address for CGSP use

Please check appropriate box: ❑ Resource purchased by church ❑ Resource purchased by self ❑ Other

CHURCH INFORMATION

Church Name

Address (Street, Route, or P.O. Box)	City, State, or Province	Zip/Postal Code

CHANGE REQUEST ONLY

☐ Former Name

☐ Former Address	City, State, or Province	Zip/Postal Code
☐ Former Church	City, State, or Province	Zip/Postal Code

Signature of Pastor, Conference Leader, or Other Church Leader	Date

*New participants are requested but not required to give SS# and date of birth. Existing participants, please give CGSP# when using SS# for the first time. Thereafter, only one ID# is required. **Mail to:** Christian Growth Study Plan, One LifeWay Plaza, Nashville, TN 37234-0117. Fax: (615)251-5067.

Revised 4-05

1 John 3:1, KJV
"Behold, what manner of love the Father hath bestowed upon us, that we should be called the sons of God."

1 John 3:1, HCSB
"Look at how great a love the Father has given us, that we should be called God's children."

Hebrews 10:24-25, KJV
"Let us consider one another to provoke unto love and to good works: Not forsaking the assembling of ourselves together, as the manner of some is; but exhorting one another: and so much the more, as ye see the day approaching."

Hebrews 10:24-25, HCSB
"Let us be concerned about one another in order to promote love and good works, not staying away from our meetings, as some habitually do, but encouraging each other, and all the more as you see the day drawing near."

Romans 12:4-5, KJV
"As we have many members in one body, and all members have not the same office: So we, being many, are one body in Christ, and every one members one of another."

Romans 12:4-5, HCSB
"As we have many parts in one body, and all the parts do not have the same function, in the same way we who are many are one body in Christ and individually members of one another."

1 John 1:7, KJV
"If we walk in the light, as he is in the light, we have fellowship one with another, and the blood of Jesus Christ his Son cleanseth us from all sin."

1 John 1:7, HCSB
"If we walk in the light as He Himself is in the light, we have fellowship with one another, and the blood of Jesus His Son cleanses us from all sin."

John 13:34, KJV
"A new commandment I give unto you, That ye love one another; as I have loved you, that ye also love one another."

John 13:34, HCSB
"I give you a new commandment: love one another. Just as I have loved you, you must also love one another."

Galatians 6:2, KJV
"Bear ye one another's burdens, and so fulfil the law of Christ."

Galatians 6:2, HCSB
"Carry one another's burdens; in this way you will fulfill the law of Christ."

Fellowship with Believers, Week 1
1 John 3:1, HCSB

Fellowship with Believers, Week 1
1 John 3:1, KJV

Fellowship with Believers, Week 2
Hebrews 10:24-25, HCSB

Fellowship with Believers, Week 2
Hebrews 10:24-25, KJV

Fellowship with Believers, Week 3
Romans 12:4-5, HCSB

Fellowship with Believers, Week 3
Romans 12:4-5, KJV

Fellowship with Believers, Week 4
1 John 1:7, HCSB

Fellowship with Believers, Week 4
1 John 1:7, KJV

Fellowship with Believers, Week 5
John 13:34, HCSB

Fellowship with Believers, Week 5
John 13:34, KJV

Fellowship with Believers, Week 6
Galatians 6:2, HCSB

Fellowship with Believers, Week 6
Galatians 6:2, KJV